国家文物局
主编

中国
重要考古发现

文物出版社
2006 · 5

图书在版编目(CIP)数据

2005 中国重要考古发现／国家文物局编．－北京：
文物出版社，2006.5
ISBN 7－5010－1903－7

Ⅰ.2…　Ⅱ.国…　Ⅲ.考古发现－中国－2005
Ⅳ.K87

中国版本图书馆 CIP 数据核字(2006)第 032187 号

2005 中国重要考古发现

国家文物局　主编

文物出版社出版发行

北京五四大街 29 号
http://www.wenwu.com
E-mail　web@wenwu.com
北京圣彩虹制版印刷技术有限公司制版印刷
2006 年 5 月第一版　2006 年 5 月第一次印刷
787 × 1092　1/16　印张：12
ISBN 7－5010－1903－7/K · 1001
定价：80 元

State Administration of
Cultural Heritage

MAJOR ARCHAEOLOGICAL
DISCOVERIES IN

Cultural Relics Publishing House

Beijing 2006

协作单位

中国社会科学院考古研究所
中国国家博物馆
故宫博物院
北京市文物研究所
天津市文化遗产保护中心
河北省文物研究所
山西省考古研究所
南京博物院
浙江省文物考古研究所
江西省文物考古研究所
山东省文物考古研究所
河南省文物考古研究所
湖南省文物考古研究所
陕西省考古研究所
甘肃省文物考古研究所
新疆文物考古研究所
北京大学考古文博学院
大同市考古研究所
南京市博物馆
扬州市文物考古队
景德镇陶瓷考古研究所
洛阳市文物工作队
洛阳市第二文物工作队
长沙市文物考古研究所
西安市文物保护考古所
《文物》编辑部

目 录 CONTENTS

前言 PREFACE

2005年国家文物局审批考古发掘项目600余项,我们以各地的考古工作汇报为依据,结合考古研究机构和专家的推荐意见,遴选出34项本年度重要考古发现,编辑成册,以飨读者。

浙江嵊州小黄山遗址是新石器时代早期文化遗存,其体现的文化面貌不同于跨湖桥文化和河姆渡文化,为研究人类文明从采集经济到农耕经济的过渡与转变提供了丰富的资料。河南灵宝西坡遗址仰韶文化中期墓地与壕沟的发现,为了解西坡遗址的文化内涵、规模和聚落内部形态提供了新的资料。浙江桐乡姚家山贵族墓葬是浙北地区近年来发现的最高级别的良渚文化墓地,出土大量玉、石、陶、牙骨器等珍贵文物,有两类玉器为正式考古发掘中首次发现。

南水北调一期工程2005年度控制性文物保护项目顺利开展,考古工作成果丰硕。河北唐县北放水遗址是近年来先商考古的重大收获,对廓清该地区夏时期考古学文化面貌有着重要意义。河南鹤壁刘庄遗址发现大批仰韶文化晚期大司空类型遗迹、遗物以及较大规模的下七垣文化墓地。下七垣文化墓地共发现墓葬336座,出土器物近500件,这是中原地区首次发现如此规模的夏时期公共墓地,为先商文化的发掘研究工作填补了空白,为研究墓葬制度、社会结构、商人渊源、夏商关系等学术问题提供了重要的实物资料。

山西绛县横水镇西周墓地的考古工作取得重大收获,共发现墓葬300余座,清理110余座,出土随葬器物有铜、陶、蚌、贝、漆、玉器等,共206件组。从西周中期的倗伯夫人墓中,发现了十分珍贵的荒帷遗迹,并及时实施了保护搬迁。陕西韩城梁带村墓地是关中东部首次发现的两周之际的诸侯国墓地,保存状况较好。通过调查勘探共发现两周时期墓葬103

座、车马坑17座，从抢救性发掘的3座墓葬的形制、规模和随葬品推断，其应该是诸侯级墓葬。

通过对甘肃礼县鸾亭山汉代祭祀遗址的考古发掘，发现祭祀坑、犬祭坑等遗迹，出土玉器、骨器、瓦当70余件，丰富了人们对汉代祭祀相关礼制的认识。山西大同沙岭北魏壁画墓画面保存好，内容丰富，发现漆片上的墨书文字显示，这是已知北魏时期最早的纪年墓。唐大明宫丹凤门遗址的考古发掘工作取得重要成果，5个门道的发现澄清了相关学术难题，促进了中国古代都城的考古研究。

边疆地区考古方面，位于罗布泊西南荒漠中的小河墓地几年来累计发掘墓葬167座，出土珍贵文物数以千计，初步推测小河墓地的年代大致在公元前2000年左右。新疆和田地区于田县阿羌乡流水墓地，是首次于昆仑山北麓发现的青铜时代墓葬，为研究昆仑山地区距今3000年前后的文化面貌提供了新资料。

水下考古方面，福建东海平潭碗礁 I 号沉船出水康熙中期景德镇民窑瓷器17000余件，为古代造船史、陶瓷史及海上丝绸之路的研究提供了丰富的资料。

近年来，我国经济飞速发展，国家对文物保护工作的支持力度也越来越大。2005年的考古工作主要是围绕学术课题研究、大遗址保护工程以及基本建设中的文物保护工作开展的。一年来，全国的考古工作者通过辛勤工作和不懈努力为我们献上了完美的答卷。我们编发此册快报，是希望更多的人来关注我国文物保护事业，积极贯彻落实国务院关于加强文化遗产保护工作的通知精神，为构建社会主义和谐社会贡献力量。

河南许昌灵井旧石器时代晚期遗址首次发掘

FIRST EXCAVATION ON THE LATE PALEOLITHIC SITE AT LINGJING IN XUCHANG, HENAN

灵井遗址位于许昌市西北约 15 公里的灵井镇西侧，1965 年，古人类学家周国兴先生从村民挖井挖出距地表深约 10 米的堆积物中采集到一批动物化石、细小石器及打制石器。材料发表在《考古》1974 年第 2 期，认为灵井遗址为"中石器时代"的代表遗址，引起了考古界的重视。但在之后的 40 年中，灵井泉水一直处于喷涌状态，出露地层全部被水域覆盖。2005 年 4 月，因附近煤矿透水，致使灵井等一批泉水断流，河南省文物考古研究所报请省和国家文物行政主管部门批准，会同许昌市文物部门对这处重要的史前文化遗址进行抢救性发掘。

发掘时间从 2005 年 6 月至 12 月底，在 40 × 2 平方米的范围内，共发掘出旧石器时代晚期石器、骨器制品 4000 余件，其中磨制石器和骨器 30 件，并首次发现旧石器时代晚期的磨制雕刻器。

距地表深 4.8 米的地层中，文化遗物集中在上下两层沉积物中出土。上文化层（湖相沉积）分布在灵井泉附近，为橘黄色粉砂土，土质纯净，胶结较重，遍布铁锰氧化斑点。粉砂土的顶部有 20～40 厘米的钙板层。

上文化层出土的石器有砾石石器和细小石器两种。砾石石器约占石器总量的 20% 左右。石料主要为各类石英岩，尺寸较大，同南方主工业和洛河上、中游代表石器类似。经初步分类观察，石器类型有石核、石片、砍砸器、刮削器和石锤。典型的石锤一般由石核转化而来，原料为石英质。石器个体较小，个别标本在 1 平方厘米以下，重在 0.5～1 克范围内，可称得上"微型石器"，且制作精细，技术精湛。多数标本在石料的一边或一端加工，其他部位一般不作修理，形状多不规则。细小石器原料以石英为主。石器类型有雕刻器、各式刮削器和尖状器。雕刻器较为典型，数量较多，有屋脊形雕刻器和斜边雕刻器等种类。国内占数量较多的圆头刮削器在该地层中数量较少。精细加工的石器多用小砾石石片或石核做成，不少标本上分布有砾石面。传统观点认为南北方石器工业的区别是，南方为大型砾石石器工业，北方为石片石器和小型石器工业，虽然两种工业技术在灵井并存，但不能仅看到灵井处于南北方的过渡地带，石器原料决定技术的因素尤其不能低估。

下文化层上部为漫滩相向湖相过渡，灰黄色黏土质粉砂土，富含柱形纵向分布的结核，中有空隙，为上层水分渗透的通道。下部为一套浅灰色湖

T2剖面（上部为钙板）
Section of Test Square T2 (calcium layer at top)

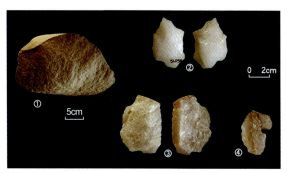

上文化层出土石制品
Lithic Products from Upper Cultural Layer

下文化层出土石核
Stone Cores from Lower Cultural Layer

相沉积物，地层由北向南倾斜，层理分界不明显。同上文化层比较，大型砾石石器明显减少，局部磨制的石器和骨器增多，并有大量使用痕迹的骨器出土。其中一件典型的磨刃屋脊形雕刻器，为国内仅见。有些石核台面有磨擦痕迹，以局部磨制为主，台面通体磨制仅一件，并发现有用燧石核工作面作

磨器的标本，这种情况在全国同类遗存中似不多见。在出土的骨料上80%以上有人工痕迹，磨制骨器主要出土于下文化层下部。经初步观察，磨制骨器主要集中在尖、刃部位，有些制成小雕刻器。作为间接制法的中介物和压制法修理石器的工具，在该遗址中也有发现，一般用鹿角和食肉动物的胫骨

刮削器
Scraper

尖状器
Point

石核
Stone Core

雕刻器（4个面）
Burin (four facets)

顶端为材料，这类器物在其他遗址中似不曾见到。截尾技术普遍使用，部分标本有明显的使用痕迹。下文化层文化遗物由上而下有逐步增多趋势，该层深度不详。

灵井遗址出土的动物化石主要有牛、野马、野猪、赤鹿、啮齿类、鸟类等20余种。以食草动物和杂食动物为主，肉食动物较少，仅在骨制的工具中见到。出土的骨骼多有人工痕迹，以取肉和加工工具痕迹为主，另筛洗出大量制作工具的骨渣、碎片。骨骼以牙齿、椎骨、趾骨、肋骨居多，长骨除骨器和加工废料以外几乎不见。有些标本出土时周围分布有零星的石片，骨骼的划痕同石片刃缘一致，应为剔肉所遗留。

在距遗址西7公里处地层3米下发现一段古河道，细砂中含大量石英岩砾石，可能是灵井石器原料产地之一。

寻找新旧石器时代的过渡类型文化是当前史前考古的一项重要课题，在华北，旧石器文化结束和早期新石器文化出现之间大约有2000年的文化缺失。灵井遗址文化层上部的钙板层应是区域环境和气候的标志，它同大岗遗址的黑炉土、南阳盆地上部地层中的结核砾石层和灵井遗址周围地层广泛出露的小砾石结核层一样，应为全新世气候转暖的产物，可判定为更新世和全新世的界面，倘若如此，灵井遗址最晚应在距今1万年以前，这一点从某些出土的动物化石属更新世的灭绝种得到印证。从地层上观察，灵井的钙板层同新石器文化层中间有约

3米厚的地层，既不包含新石器遗物，也不见旧石器时代遗物，这可能是代表猎人文化的灵井人随着全新世气候转暖而北上，而南方来的新石器早期文化，循着砾石文化向北传播的路线到达本区之前的缺环。

灵井遗址是国内首次发掘的以泉水为中心，包括湖相、漫滩相（湿地）堆积物为背景的旧石器时代晚期遗址，是人类狩猎、肢解动物、加工兽皮、石器、骨器的工作营地，属原地埋藏类型。它优于洞穴堆积的狭小和河流阶地堆积的散漫，以及因二次搬运所造成的混乱。灵井遗址是华北地区文化遗物和包涵信息最丰富的遗址之一，它有着较大面积的原生地层和丰富的遗物，相信随着工作的深入，可能会确定该遗址在探讨某些重大学术问题中举足轻重的地位。

（供稿：李占扬）

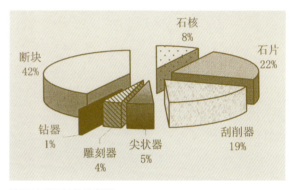

脉石英质石制品分类图
Typology of Vein Quartz Products

地层中石器分布
Distribution of Lithic Products
in Deposit

动物化石
Animal Fossils

The Lingjing site is located west of Lingjing Town in Xuchang City, Henan Province. The 2005 excavation opened an area of 260 sq m, unearthing cultural remains from the upper and the lower layers of lacustrine deposition. Within the excavated area, 2,452 lithic products and about 3,000 animal fossils (including artificial bone implements) were unearthed.

Lithic products were made of either large quartz rocks or small vein quartz gravel, and the lithic finds consisted of finished implements, cores, flakes and broken chunks. In flaking and chipping, the technique of hammer percussion was primarily employed, but the flock-on-block technique was also occasionally used. Most blanks were broken pieces and broken chunks with irregular shapes, but some delicately worked microlithic implements were also present. Comparatively, vein quartz products were mainly composed of scrapers, although there were some points, burins, and awls;

quartz products, however, were mainly chopping tools. Therefore, the lithic products made of two rock materials became complimentary. Because vein quartz gravel was the more abundant material, small lithic products consequently were dominant in quantity in the lithic assemblage. The lithic industry at Lingjing presents general characteristics of the Paleolithic industry of north China, but some gravel choppers also reflected elements of southern Paleolithic industry.

There were over 20 species of unearthed animal fossils, and most of them belong to Salawusu Faunas. The unearthed fossils contain a large amount of bone implements, which were either directly chipped or burnished, bearing traces of use occasionally. Judging from aspects of stratigraphy, remain types, and paleoenvironment, the lithic products from the 2005 excavation should belong to the late Paleolithic period.

北京东胡林遗址
2005 年发掘又获重要成果

FURTHER IMPORTANT ACHIEVEMENTS FROM THE 2005 EXCAVATION AT THE DONGHULIN SITE, BEIJING

东胡林遗址位于北京市门头沟区斋堂镇东胡林村村西，清水河北岸的三级阶地上，是重要的新石器时代早期遗址。该遗址发现于1966年，1995年北京市公布为地下文物埋藏区。经国家文物局批准，由北京大学考古文博学院和北京市文物研究所共同组成的东胡林考古发掘队曾于2001年和2003年先后对东胡林遗址进行了两次发掘，出土了比较丰富的打制石器、细石器及大量的动物遗骸和一定数量的陶片、骨器、蚌器等文化遗物。发现的遗迹有分布密集的火塘、石器加工场所以及一座完整的新石器时代早期墓葬。保存完好的古人类遗骸的发现填补了北京地区乃至华北地区自山顶洞人、田园洞人（距今约3～2万年）以来，人类发展史的一段空白。经北京大学考古文博学院科技考古与文物保护实验室测定，东胡林人及其文化遗存的年代在距今1万年前后，属新石器时代早期。

2005 年 8～11 月，东胡林考古队对遗址进行了第三次发掘。此次发掘又获重要成果，出土一批丰富的文化遗物，包括打制石器、细石器、小型磨制石器、陶器、骨器、蚌器、赤铁矿颜料，以及数量较多的鹿、猪等动物的骨骼（包括烧骨）和大型蚌壳等。此外，还发现了灰坑、火塘、墓葬及居住遗迹，并浮选出了丰富的动植物遗存。这次发现的一座保存完好的墓葬及鱼鳔、骨梗刀、赤铁矿颜料等文化遗存，为研究东胡林人及其文化又增添了新资料。

此次发现的新石器时代早期墓葬，系土坑竖穴墓，葬式为屈肢葬。在墓主人的头部发现随葬的一件磨光小型石斧，颈部及胸腹部发现有多枚穿孔小螺壳，应为墓主人生前佩挂使用之物。

本次发掘的另一重要收获是在原东胡林文化层之下又发现了时代更早的打制石器及烧火遗迹，为

T19 北壁剖面
North–wall Profile of Test Square T19

烧火后遗留的灰堆
Remaining Ash after Firing

墓葬
Burial

打制石器
Chipped Stone Implement

小型磨制石器
Small Polished Stone Implement

细石刻和细石叶
Microlithic Burins and Blades

石刃骨梗刀
Bone Knife-base with Stone Blade

骨鱼镖
Bone Harpoon

可复原的陶器
Restorable Pottery Ware

寻找时代更早的古人类及其文化遗存提供了重要线索。

浮选出的丰富的动植物遗存，为探讨北方地区粟类旱作农业及家畜起源，研究北京地区新石器时代早期人类的生存环境与人地关系，进而探索华北地区新、旧石器时代过渡问题提供了十分重要的新资料。

（供稿：赵朝洪 王涛 员雪梅 崔天兴 郁金城 郭京宁）

The Donghulin site, an important site dating to the early Neolithic, is located on the tertiary terrace of the northern bank of the Qingshuihe River which lies to the west of Donghulin village in Zhaitang, Mentougou district, Beijing. During the field season from August to November 2005, the archaeological team organized by the School of Archaeology and Museology of Beijing (Peking) University and Beijing Institute of Cultural Relics carried out the third excavation at the site. The unearthed rich cultural remains include chipped stone implements, microlithic wares, small polished stone tools, pottery wares, bone implements, shell implements, red ocher pigment as well as a large amount of deer and pig bones (including burned ones) and large shells. In addition, the identified feature types include ash pit, fire place, burial and residential place. Furthermore, rich animal and plant remains were collected through a water floatation process. The discoveries of the 2005 excavation, e.g. the intact burial, bone harpoon, bone knife-base with stone blade and red ocher pigment, provide additional data for the study of the Donghulin people and their culture.

浙江嵊州小黄山遗址发掘

THE XIAOHUANGSHAN SITE IN SHENGZHOU, ZHEJIANG

小黄山遗址位于浙江省嵊州市甘霖镇上杜山村。1984年嵊州市文物管理处文物普查时发现，确定为良渚文化遗址。2005年元月，浙江省文物考古研究所在曹娥江流域史前文化遗址专题考古调查时，发现该遗址下部堆积为新石器时代较早阶段遗存。经国家文物局批准，省文物考古研究所会同嵊州市文物管理处于2005年3月开始对小黄山遗址进行抢救性考古发掘，先后布方近2000平方米，已清理灰坑、墓葬、房基等遗迹单位150余个，出土石器、可复原陶器近1000件和大量的陶片标本。

小黄山遗址坐落于相对高度10米左右的古台地上，遗址周围是曹娥江上游长乐江宽阔的河谷平原，依山面水，地理环境十分优越。调查勘探确认，小黄山遗址原有面积5万多平方米，是长江中下游地区新石器时代中期早段规模最大的聚落遗址。

发掘布方分A、B两个区域3个地点，A区在东、B区在西，相距约170米。

A区一期遗存

遗迹主要有灰坑、墓葬、房基等。灰坑多为方形、圆形的深土坑，坑壁陡直规整，坑底平整，直径（边长）1米上下。坑内堆积遗物很少，很可能是为储藏采集块茎植物、坚果而挖建的储藏坑。AH14、AH19坑口一侧营建成斜坡状，坑底铺垫块石或残磨盘。坑底置放石磨盘，很可能与食物加工场所有关。AH15长方形土坑比较规整，坑内东侧5件夹砂红陶釜、1件陶杯竖向整齐排放，很可能属特殊用途的祭祀坑。已发现墓葬10余座，散落于居址周围，多为长方形竖穴土坑墓，墓坑东西向居多，人骨无存。少量日用陶器随葬，敞口小平底盆、圈足罐、平底高颈壶为常见随葬陶器。AM1、AM2两墓保存较好。房基由柱坑、基槽组成，已初步确定的三处房基均为南北向布列，似可分间并发现营建时对场地进行平整和铺垫的迹象。

出土遗物几乎全为陶器、石器，有机质遗物由于酸性埋藏环境很难保存。

出土陶器，夹砂红衣陶占绝大多数，胎壁粗厚，制作原始。平底器、圈足器为主，圜底器不多，不见三足器。敞口小平底盆、大平底盘、镂孔圈足盘、圈足钵、圈足罐、平底高颈壶、圜底釜为基本

小黄山遗址 A 区发掘现场
Excavation in District A of the Xiaohuangshan Site

陶器群。部分盆、盘类陶器口沿为多角形。少量陶器口沿部有锯齿形装饰,部分罐类陶器口沿外侧刻划网格纹,绳纹少见。陶器口沿、肩腹部流行把手（鋬）。

石器制造打制、磨制工艺兼用并存。打制石器有砍砸器、尖状器、刮削器等。磨制石器数量不多,截面椭圆形的石斧多见,通体磨制,残损严重。石磨石、石磨盘是出土数量最多的石器,不同形态的磨石、石锤与石磨盘配合使用。穿孔石器及带凹槽的石球也颇具特色,用途值得研究。

A 区二期遗存

灰沟堆积。石器种类、形制变化不是很大。陶器中夹砂灰陶为主,少量夹炭陶。夹炭红衣陶红色艳丽,夹炭黑陶黑色乌黑纯正。夹砂灰陶圜底釜、双鼻与口部齐平的平底罐、平底盆、平底盘、钵、小杯、器盖常见。釜饰绳纹流行;大平底器盖手捏成型,外壁残存制作陶器时草刮痕迹。

B 区一期遗存

遗迹主要是灰坑,形态和 A 区基本相同,没有发现坑底置放石磨盘的灰坑。BH12 直径达 1.9 米,容积近 3 立方米; BH9、BH10、BH17 等三灰坑紧密相连并落在一个更大的浅坑内,大坑套小坑。BH12 坑周围发现分布比较有规则的柱坑遗迹,推测坑上当有简陋棚蓬建筑覆盖。在 BH12 下方还发现烧火遗迹。

出土石器、陶器种类和形态与 A 区基本相同。最为完整的一件石磨盘重达 30 公斤。还发现石雕

A 区一期 H14
Pit H14 of Period I in District A

A区一期H15
Pit H15 of Period I in
District A

人首一件，高7.6厘米，形象传神。

B区二期遗存

与B区一期遗存比较，文化面貌传承发展的特征十分明确，演变轨迹清晰。BM2是该期比较典型的墓葬，长方形竖穴土坑，墓坑东西向，随葬夹砂红陶平底罐、夹炭红衣陶圈足盆各1件，夹炭红衣陶圈足盆下发现一片残损腐蚀很严重的颅骨。夹砂黑衣陶开始出现，有趣的是红衣、黑衣共存于同一件陶器上，蕴示陶器烧制技术有了明显变化。夹砂陶器胎壁趋薄。基本陶器群依然是敞口小平底盆、大平底盘、圈足盘、圈足罐、平底高颈壶、圜底釜。新出现敛口圜底钵、双腹豆、夹砂灰陶折肩卵腹绳纹釜、甑等器形，绳纹装饰数量明显增加，出现交错绳纹、镂孔放射线和红底白彩等新因素。新出现的陶器形制与萧山跨湖桥类型文化同类陶器十分相似，装饰风格也基本一致，尤以坞垄篷发掘点遗存为典型。从陶器成型方法、装饰手法等方面表现出更为古老原始的文化特征。

小黄山遗址A区、B区第一期遗存文化面貌、内涵特征完全相同。A区一、二期堆积层位上直接叠压，文化面貌存在一定的差异，而文化内涵内在联系十分密切。B区一、二期层位上直接叠压，陶器种类、形制传承发展的逻辑关系十分清楚，文化内涵演变脉络清晰。A区二期和B区二期层位上没

有直接的叠压打破关系，文化面貌、内涵特征也有一定的区别，这是个耐人寻味值得探讨的问题。

小黄山遗址新石器时代较早阶段遗存地层叠压

A区一期M5
Tomb M5 of Period I in District A

夹砂红衣陶豆
Reddish Sandy Pottery
dou-plate on Pedestal

夹砂红衣陶平底盆
Red-coated Sandy Pottery
pen-basin with Flat Bottom

夹砂红衣陶圈足盘
Red-coated Sandy Pottery
dou-plate on Pedestal

夹砂灰陶绳纹釜
Cord-marked Greyish Sandy
fu-cooking pot

夹细砂红衣陶长颈壶
Red-coated Fine Sandy Pottery
hu-pot with Long Neck

夹砂陶绳纹圈足罐
Cord-marked Sandy Pottery
guan-jar on Ring-foot

夹砂红衣陶甑
Red-coated Sandy Pottery
zeng-steamer

夹炭黑陶豆
Black Pottery *dou*-plate on Pedestal with Carbonized Paste

夹砂陶豆
Sandy Pottery *dou*-plate on
Pedestal

关系明确，早晚传承演变轨迹清晰，系同一文化的不同发展阶段。经北京大学考古文博院科技考古与文物保护实验室对B区一期的3个木炭标本的¹⁴C测定经树轮校正值均在7000BC左右；A区二期的3个木炭标本的¹⁴C测定经树轮校正值均超过6000BC，而位于沟底的夹炭陶标本¹⁴C测年校正值超过6800BC。坳垄篷1个木炭标本的¹⁴C测年校正值为5700BC上下。根据小黄山遗存文化面貌，结合¹⁴C测年数据，我们认为小黄山遗存的相对年代距今9000～7700年上下是可信的。

小黄山遗存呈现的是一种新石器时代较早阶段新颖地域文化，是一支分布于钱塘江中上游丘陵地区，依托动植物等食物资源丰富的生态环境，以采集、狩猎为主要生业形态兼营农耕的不同于跨湖桥、河姆渡的新的考古学文化。小黄山遗址为人类文化从采集经济到农耕经济的过渡与转变、农业起源与发展的机制、模式的探讨提供了一个内涵丰富的范例。

（供稿：王海明 张恒 杨卫）

石刀
Stone Knife

石雕人首
Stone Human Head Sculpture

穿孔石器
Perforated Stone Implement

The Xiaohuangshan site is located at Shangdushancun village in Ganlin, Shengzhou City, Zhejiang Province. The original size of this site is over 50,000 sq m and is the largest settlement in the middle and lower Changjiang River branches dated to the early phase of the middle Neolithic period.

The Zhejiang Provincial Institute of Archaeology excavated the Xiaohuangshan site in 2005. The early mid-Neolithic remains of the site are rich and tentatively classified into two periods. The features from Period I include the following types: pit, groove, storage pit, and burial. Storage pits were either round or square in shape, or were with a sloping passage. In some storage pits, damaged stone mortars were placed at the bottom. Burials were all rectangular shallow pits and mostly in the east-west direction. The pottery assemblage of Period I mainly consists of sandy wares with red coating, including types of the *pen*-basin, *pan*-plate, *bo*-bow, *guan*-jar, *fu*-cooking pot, and *hu*-pot. Of the lithic artifacts of Period I, mortars, chunk-shaped millstones, hammers, axes, adzes, perforated implements, and grooved spheres are common. In addition, a stone human head was found with lively carvings. Comparatively, the types of pottery and lithic artifacts of Period II are basically the same as those of the earlier period, but there is a larger amount of greyish sandy wares. The newly appeared pottery types include the *bo*-bowl with contracted mouth, dou-plate on pedestal with double-layered body, cord-marked and egg-shaped greyish sandy *fu*-cooking pot with angular body, and *zeng*-steamer. The cord-marked surface pattern also became popular.

At the Xiaohuangshan site, the deposit is thick, cultural remains are rich, the stratigraphy of the early and late strata is clear, the development process is evident, and cultural tradition is continuous without remarkable variation. Therefore, the early and late remains are two developing steps of the same archaeological culture. According to the result of calibrated ^{14}C dating, which was performed by the Laboratory of Scientific Archaeology and Heritage Conservation of Beijing (Peking) University, the Xiaohuangshan site is approximately 7,700 to 9,000 years old.

13

湖南洪江
高庙遗址发掘

EXCAVATION OF THE GAOMIAO SITE
IN HONGJIANG, HUNAN

高庙遗址是一处典型的贝丘遗址，1991年对该遗址第一次发掘的部分资料公布后，引起了国内外学术界的极大关注，为了更全面地了解该遗址的文化内涵和整体情况，湖南省文物考古研究所分别于2004年和2005年又相继对其进行了两次发掘，前后三次发掘揭露的总面积近1700平方米。

该遗址位于湖南西部洪江市（原黔阳县）安江镇东北约5公里的岔头乡岩里村，地处沅水北岸的一级台地上，分布面积约3万平方米。

通过对该遗址前后三次发掘，获知遗址顶部的地层堆积较薄，厚度在0.8～1.5米左右，主要为史前居民住宅、祭祀场所和茔地。其周围则为斜坡，是贝丘堆积的主要场所，堆积厚度达3.5～6.5米左右。

遗址的新石器时代文化堆积分为下、上两大部分，分属于两个不同的考古学文化：其中下部地层所处的年代约为距今7800～6800年左右，文化特征明显有别于周邻地区同时期的考古学文化，鉴于具下部地层相同文化特征的遗存在本区域的辰溪、

中方和麻阳县等多个地点均有出土，区域特征鲜明，但又以高庙遗址所出最为典型，且属最先发现，故以本遗址为名将其命名为"高庙文化"。高庙遗址上部地层堆积现暂称为高庙上层遗存，亦在此区域多个县市的遗址中发现有相同特征的遗存，其年代约为距今6300～5300年左右。

高庙下部地层遗存中揭示的房屋均为挖洞立柱的排架式木构地面建筑，多为长方形两开间和三开间的结构，方向朝东或朝东南，面积20～40平方米不等。房屋附近还设有窖穴。墓葬流行竖穴土坑侧身屈肢葬，头朝东，面北。墓底无随葬品，仅在填土中填埋少量石片石器和兽骨，但在一座墓的人骨架下发现有编织成方孔的竹席。2005年在遗址顶部揭示了一处距今约7000年左右的大型祭祀场所，已揭露面积700多平方米。整个祭祀遗迹呈南北中轴线布局，由主祭（司仪）场所、祭祀坑以及与祭祀场所的附属建筑——议事或休息的房子及其附设的窖穴共三部分组成。其中主祭（司仪）部位在整个祭祀场所的北部，由四个主柱洞组成两两对称、略呈扇形的排架式"双阙"式建筑。双阙的

东、西两侧分别有一个和两个侧柱。祭祀坑共发现39个，均位于司仪场所的南方。房子为两室一厨结构，在主祭部位的西侧，面积约40平方米，门朝东。窖穴则分别位于厨房门外东侧以及祭仪场所的右前方。

下部地层遗存出土的石器以各型砍砸器和用作刮削工具的各类石片石器，以及大量的扁平亚腰形石网坠最具特色，绝大部分用锤击法单面打制而成，继承了本区域旧石器时代中晚期"沅水文化类群"遗存的技术传统。此外还出土了大量的石球，以及石磨盘、磨棒、石锤、石砧和砺石等，而磨制石器如斧、锛、凿等数量很少。与石器伴出的骨（刀、匕、针、锥、簪和刻纹牌饰等）、牙（锥、象牙雕饰）和蚌器（皆穿孔，当为挂饰或蚌刀）均经精磨和抛光。所出陶器皆手制，器壁厚薄较均匀，器形规整。出土了我国目前所知年代最早的精美白陶制品，纹饰繁缛。陶器造型主要是圜底和圈足

器，不见三足器和尖底器。器类主要有釜、罐、盘、钵、簋、碗和杯等，其中罐类器尤为丰富。陶器装饰是高庙下部地层遗存中最突出的特征之一。釜、罐和钵类器的器腹多饰绳纹，而在罐的颈、肩部，钵、盘和簋形器的上腹部通常都饰由戳印篦点纹组成的各种图案，最具代表性者为形态各异的鸟纹、獠牙兽面纹、太阳纹和八角星纹，另有平行带状纹、连线波折纹、连续梯形纹、垂幛纹和圈点纹。同时，还出现了朱红色或黑色的矿物颜料的彩绘和填彩。

高庙上层遗存的房屋继承了高庙文化时期的排架式木构地面建筑及其结构，门多朝南，已出现木骨泥墙的作法。墓葬的葬式仍保留有屈肢葬的传统，头多朝东，新出现了成人仰身直肢葬和儿童瓮棺葬等新葬式。另外发现了首领夫妻并穴墓，其中男性墓（M27）随葬玉戚和石刨形斧各一件，女性墓（M26）随葬玉璜、玉玦和象牙。

"高庙文化"陶罐
Pottery *guan*-jar, Gaomiao Culture

"高庙文化"大型祭祀场所
Grand Sacrificial Plaza of the Gaomiao Culture

高庙上层遗存中以打制砍斫器和刮削石片石器为主体的生产工具,从原料的采集到制作方式,均继承了高庙文化的技术传统,磨制石器依然只占很小的比例。有所变化的是,已不见亚腰形网坠,但新出现了双肩石斧、弧刃石刀、圭形石凿和薄体的石铲等器物,并出土有重达13.5斤的巨型石斧,出现了石器的切割、穿孔和抛光技术。其他质地的用具有陶纺轮、骨拍、骨锥、骨匕和骨针等,并且有骨簪、玉璜、玉玦、石璜、石牌饰和野猪獠牙等装饰品。陶器的制作方式大都为手制轮修,泥条盘筑与贴片法并存,并已出现慢轮制作技术。釜、罐等大件器物的内壁常见凹凸不平的指窝。小件器物或器物的圈足、鼎腿以及支脚等附件均系手制分做,陶系以夹砂褐红陶、红陶和褐陶为主,偶见白陶。与“高庙文化”遗存的显著区别是部分陶器的颜色呈内黑而外红,伴出一定数量的泥质红陶,器表多经打磨或绘有彩饰。陶器造型虽仍以圜底器和圈足器为主,但出现了三足器(鼎)、尖底器(缸),以及大量的支脚。主要器类有釜、罐、钵、盆、盘、

豆、碗和支脚等,其中的窄沿釜、盆形釜、大口罐、宽沿彩陶罐、圜底钵、圈足碗和盘等是最具代表性的器物,器型与“高庙文化”遗存所出迥异,而在其年代较晚的遗迹中出土的泥质黑陶薄胎曲腹杯、簋和壶等器物已完全属于大溪文化的遗存。陶器装饰的最大特点是:釜、罐、钵类器物的腹部盛行凸点纹,器颈则饰粗篦片戳印纹,分别构成如梯格、带状、曲折、雪花、麦穗、雨线纹等图案,部分罐颈则刻划网格或斜、竖线组合图案,支脚常饰按窝,豆、碗等器物的圈足上多饰镂孔或锥点。绝大部分的泥质红陶宽沿罐皆施有暗红或白色陶衣,其上彩绘带状、波浪、网格、涡纹或勾线等图案,颜色有赭褐、深红、黑、白四色。此外,在蛋壳陶杯的外壁也饰有彩绘图案。上部地层遗存的基本特征表明它是洞庭湖区的大溪文化向本区域扩张后与当地原有文化相融合的结果。

高庙遗址发掘所揭示的下、上两个不同考古学文化的遗存,对建立沅水中上游地区新石器时代考古学文化的谱系和年代序列特别关键。其下

“高庙文化”凤鸟纹白陶簋
White Pottery *fu*-container with
Phoenix Design, Gaomiao Culture

“高庙文化”兽面纹陶钵
Pottery *bo*-bowl with Animal
Mask Design, Gaomiao Culture

"高庙文化"陶罐肩部星象纹
Star-like Design on Shoulder of
Pottery *guan*-jar, Gaomiao Culture

"高庙文化"白陶簋外底彩绘太阳纹
Sun Design Painted on Outer Surface of Bottom
of White Pottery *fu*-container, Gaomiao Culture

高庙上层 M27 出土玉戚
Jade *qi*-ax from Tomb M27
of the Upper Layer at Gaomiao

高庙上层墓葬出土瓮棺
Urn Coffin from an Upper-layer
Tomb at Gaomiao

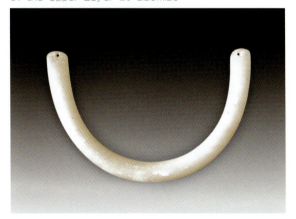

高庙上层 M26 出土玉璜
Jade *huang*-segment from Tomb
M26 of the Upper Layer at Gaomiao

高庙上层墓葬出土陶曲腹杯
Pottery Curve-bellied Cup from
an Upper-layer Tomb at Gaomiao

高庙上层四人合葬墓
Four-body Tomb of the Upper Layer at Gaomiao

部地层最早一期遗存的文化特征代表了高庙文化发生时期的基本面貌，且其生产工具的制作完全继承了本区域旧石器时代中晚期文化的技术传统，表明其文化来源于本地而不是其他区域。而上部地层遗存的文化特征一方面反映了对本区域传统文化的部分继承，另一方面又日益朝着背离本地文化且逐步地与洞庭湖区大溪文化合流的趋势发展，特别是它中晚期的遗存已完全与后者融为一体，它充分反映了洞庭湖区大溪文化向本区域的强力扩张，以及本地传统文化的崩溃和被外来文化更替的过程。

（供稿：贺刚）

The Gaomiao Site in Hongjiang City of western Hunan Province is one of the important Neolithic sites in South China. The size of the Gaomiao site is approximately 30,000 sq m and a portion of 1,700 sq m has been excavated by archaeologists from the Hunan Institute of Archaeology. The remains at the site were deposited in the upper and lower layers, each layer corresponding to a different archaeological culture.

The remains from the lower layer, which belongs to the Gaomiao Culture dated to 6,800 to 7,800 years before the present, include a large amount of tools, daily utensils, house ruins, graves, and, more importantly, a grand sacrificial plaza and many ceremonial utensils. The sacrificial plaza is composed of a series of features, including sacrificial pits, storage pits, conference halls, guest houses, etc. The ceremonial utensils comprise mainly of delicate white pottery wares incised with designs of phoenix, animal mask with protruding teeth, sun, and octagonal star.

The remains from the upper layer comprises of rich daily wares and features. The major types of feature include house structures of various kinds as well as graves of various burial types. Notably, a grave of a chief and his wife has been identified, which was furnished with delicate jades. The remains from the upper layers are similar to those from the Daxi Culture in Lake Dongting area and dated to the period of 5,300 to 6,300 years before the present.

河南灵宝西坡遗址
仰韶文化中期墓地与壕沟

MIDDLE YANGSHAO CEMETERY AND MOAT
AT THE XIPO SITE IN LINGBAO, HENAN

西坡遗址位于河南省灵宝市阳平镇西坡村西北，坐落于铸鼎原南部。遗址东、西两侧分别为沙河的支流夫夫河与灵湖河，总面积约40万平方米。河南省文物考古研究所与中国社会科学院考古研究所等单位组成联合考古队，在2000年

北壕沟
Northern Moat

10～12月、2001年3～5月、2001年11月～2002年1月和2004年4～7月曾对遗址进行了四次发掘，每次都有重大收获，引起了学术界的广泛关注。2004年10～12月，考古队对遗址进行了全面系统的钻探，初步探明了遗址的墓葬区及南、北壕沟的大体位置。为验证钻探结果，2005年4～7月，联合考古队对遗址进行了第五次发掘，发掘面积1360平方米，揭露仰韶文化中期墓葬22座，确认了北壕沟的结构和走向。

壕沟的发掘地点位于遗址东北部，发掘面积120平方米。为了解壕沟的结构和走向，发掘首先开挖了一条2×35米的南北向探沟，然后在探沟西侧、壕沟南北边沿布设了两个5×5米的探方。发掘表明，壕沟开口于西周文化层下，距地表深约2.2米。就解剖的部位看，壕沟口部宽约19.2米，从口部向下，沟壁呈约30°的缓坡，至沟宽度约13米处向下呈约75°的陡坡，底部宽约9、沟深约5.2米。沟内堆积共计16大层，自上而下分别包含了庙底沟二期、仰韶文化晚期和中期的文化堆积，其中以仰韶文化晚期的堆积最为丰厚，仰韶文化中期的堆积次之，庙底沟二期遗存最少。沟内填土中的包含物以陶片为主，石器和动物骨骼等很少。根据文化堆积及其包含物初步判断，壕沟的始建年代不晚于仰韶文化中期中段，与以前揭露的特大型房址的年代接近，属于该遗址的早期阶段。

墓葬区位于初步探明的遗址南壕沟以南约130～150米处，发掘面积1240米，揭露墓葬22座。就此次发掘看，墓葬似乎成排分布，但排列不甚规

灵宝西坡墓地鸟瞰
Top View of the Xipo
Cemetery in Lingbao

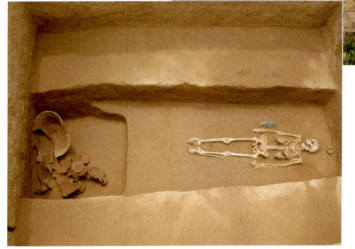

M8
Tomb M8

整，墓间距也较大。墓葬均为长方形竖穴土坑墓，无葬具，皆为单人仰身直肢葬，除一座墓主头向南且无二层台外，其余墓主均头向西或西略偏北，南北两侧都见生土二层台。个别墓葬有近似长方形的脚坑，用来放置器物。墓葬填土以黄花土为主，并掺有红褐色土和青灰色草拌泥。大部分墓葬的二层台之间的墓室由一层厚薄不一的草拌泥封盖。部分墓葬出土有陶器、石器、骨器、玉器和象牙器等随葬品。陶器多数为红陶，少数为褐陶；基本组合是釜、灶、小口瓶、钵和簋形器，一些器物的形制在以前发布的资料中少见；陶器多似专门用来随葬的明器，烧制火候低。石器有钺和不规则形石块。骨器包括簪、锥、匕、箍状器等。玉器有钺和环。象牙器有镯和箍状器。墓葬可大致分为大、中、小型墓。大型墓长 3.05～3.95、宽 2.25～3.6 米；中型墓长 2.5～2.9、宽 1.4～2.3 米；小型墓长 1.8～2.25、

宽 0.6～1.2 米。大型墓如 M8，长 3.95、宽 3.09、深 2.35 米，头顶放置一件骨质箍状器，右臂侧陈放一件长 22.9 厘米的玉钺，脚坑中随葬 9 件陶器。中型墓如 M10，长 2.6、宽 1.87、深 0.54 米，仅随葬一件残石器。小型墓如 M1，长 2.05、宽 0.95、深 0.6 米，未见随葬品。根据随葬陶器的特征初步研究，下腹有单耳、颈有凸棱的小口瓶与陕西华县太平庄 M701 随葬的泉护村一期Ⅲ段的瓶形制相似，因此推测，这批墓葬的时代大致与泉护村一期Ⅲ段大体相当，或可归入仰韶文化中期最晚阶段。

壕沟和墓地的发现，首先为了解西坡遗址的文化内涵、规模和聚落内部形态提供了新的资料，对进一步认识西坡遗址在该地区同时期聚落群中的地位及仰韶文化中期的聚落形态具有重要价值。墓地的确认是本次发掘的最重大收获。这是在仰韶文化中期的核心地区首次发现该时期的墓地。二层台的出现，风格独特的陶器，以玉器随葬，这些新鲜资料为认识仰韶文化中期的埋葬习俗、社会制度、对外文化交流等提供了十分珍贵的资料。墓葬规模及随葬品出现明显差异，表明中原地区的史前社会结构开始出现了意义深远的复杂化倾向。这无疑对于探索中原古代文明的起源、特点、进程与动因，具有重大的意义。

（供稿：马萧林 李新伟）

陶釜灶
Pottery *fu*-cauldron
and Stove

M14 出土陶器
Pottery Unearthed
from Tomb M14

M14 随葬陶器
Pottery Buried in Tomb M14

The Xipo site is located northwest of Xipo village in Yangping Town, Lingbao City, Henan Province, and approximately 400,000 sq m in size. From 2000 to 2004, four seasons of field work were carried out on the site jointly by the Henan Provincial Institute of Archaeology, the Institute of Archaeology of the Chinese Academy of Social Sciences, and other units. The fifth excavation was launched from April to July 2005, which uncovered 22 burials dated to the middle phase of the Yangshao Culture, and verified the structure and alignment of the northern moat.

The moat is underneath the deposit layer of the Western Zhou period. The moat is approximately 19.2 m wide at the opening and 9 m at the bottom, and it is 5.2 m deep. The deposit inside the moat consisted of cultural

M6 出土玉钺
Jade *yue*-ax from Tomb M6

M11 出土玉器
Jades from Tomb M11

M11 出土玉钺
Jade *yue*-ax from Tomb M11

M22 出土玉环（残）
Jade Ring from Tomb M22 (broken)

remains of a series of phases, from the middle and late periods of the Yangshao Culture to the Miaodigou II Culture. Comparatively, remains of the late Yangshao are the richest. Judging from deposit strata and associated remains, the moat was constructed no later than the middle phase of the middle period of the Yangshao Culture.

The cemetery is located approximately 130 m to 150 m south of the southern moat of the site. The exposed 22 graves were all single burials in rectangular earth pits, and none of them was buried with funerary furniture. The bodies were all placed in the extended supine position. Some graves yielded burial objects, including pottery, stone, bone, jade, and ivory artifacts. The basic composition of a funerary pottery set consists of *fu*-cooking pot, stove, small-mouthed water bottle, *bo*-bowl, and *gui*-food container. Types of stone

implements include *yue*-ax and irregular-shaped rubble. Types of bone implements include hairpin, awl, spoon, and ring-shaped object. Jades include types of *yue*-ax and *huan*-ring. Ivory implements refer to bracelet and ring-shaped object. Based on pottery morphologies, the date of the graves is probably equivalent to that of Phase III of Period 1 of the Quanhucun Culture, that is roughly the latest phase of the middle period of the Yangshao Culture.

The discovery of the moat and cemetery at Xipo has provided new data for the study of cultural appearance, site scale, and intra-settlement patterns of the Xipo site. It is also significant for a better understanding of the role and status of the Xipo site among contemporary settlements in the same region, and for the investigation of the settlement patterns of the middle Yangshao Culture.

浙江桐乡姚家山 良渚文化贵族墓葬

HIGH RANKING ARISTOCRATIC TOMBS OF THE LIANGZHU CULTURE AT YAOJIASHAN IN TONGXIANG, ZHEJIANG

姚家山遗址位于桐乡市屠甸镇荣星村南星桥组，附近良渚文化遗址分布密集，普安桥遗址即位于北部约2.5公里处。遗址中心原为一个西北－东南向分布的长方形土台，其南部有河道近东西向流过。因修筑村道和取土破坏，土台的中部和西部遭严重破坏，导致良渚大墓暴露，曾有玉璜、石钺等文物出土。

因土台被列入该市土地平整计划，2004年10月初，桐乡博物馆先行对该土墩进行调查试掘并发现良渚文化贵族墓葬。浙江省文物考古研究所经报请国家文物局同意，与桐乡博物馆组成联合考古队，于2004年11月～2005年1月，对遗址进行抢救性发掘。揭露面积共1300平方米，发现良渚文化人工堆筑的高台墓地一处，清理良渚文化高等贵族墓葬7座，祭祀坑21个。出土陶、玉、石、牙骨器等各类珍贵文物260余件（组）。

发掘和钻探表明，遗址的最下层生土为平坦的沼泽相沉积。其上有一层堆积土质细软，包含较多的动植物遗存和崧泽－良渚文化过渡时期的文化遗物，应属当时居住址附近的某种浅水或沼泽相沉积。该层上部有一层黑灰色土，显示大量植物在短期内炭化形成，其上即叠压着人工堆筑的土台。土台呈长方形覆斗状，西北－东南方向分布，现存高3.5米，顶面宽约23米左右，长度因东西部遭破坏不详，据钻探推测当在60米以上。由剖面观察，土台下部堆筑黄黑色湖沼相沉积土，土质纯净致密，不含陶片，当是取自水面以下的淤土。联系到土台南部现存的小河道，或与当时的取土活动有关。上部堆土为纯净的黄褐斑土，可能来源于濒水位置的生土。土台营筑过程大致分三阶段，在堆积相上表现为三期堆土层间夹有两层较薄的黑灰土，含有陶片和有机物，说明营建的过程中有短暂间隙。

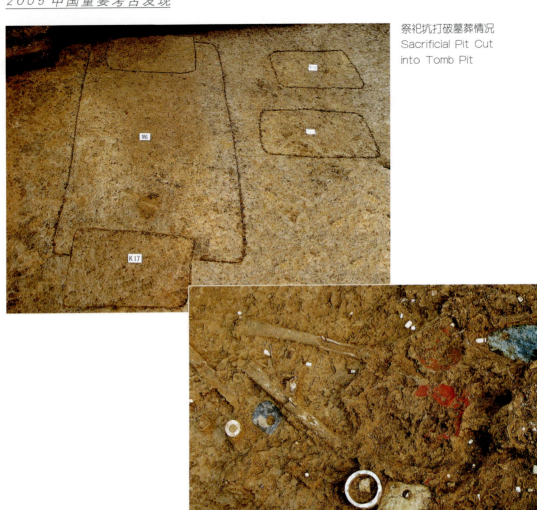

祭祀坑打破墓葬情况
Sacrificial Pit Cut
into Tomb Pit

M7 部分遗物埋葬情况
Buried Condition of Partial
Remains in Tomb M7

土台面上发现良渚文化墓葬7座、与墓葬相关的祭祀坑21个。墓葬分布于土台中部，分南北两排东西向依次排列。M1、M5为北排，M4、M2、M3、M7、M6构成南排。墓皆开口于表土下，打破土台顶面，墓向190°～205°之间，大体垂直于土台的走向。墓葬为长方形土坑竖穴墓，墓坑长度3.17～4.35、宽1.3～2米。北排两墓现存深度仅0.2米左右，南排墓葬埋藏颇深。墓内大多发现棺椁痕迹。M7中，根据土色可辨出一椁一棺。椁棺侧板可能因土层压力略向内倾。据墓底观察，椁为长方形，长3.5、宽1.47米，长板向两端各出头0.06、板厚0.05米，棺为不出头的长方形，长2.9、宽1.02米，盖板已朽，厚度不明，侧、底板

厚约0.06米。棺底两侧近前后挡板下有两根横向垫木，垫木为圆形原木，长1.3、直径0.1米，放置于墓底的浅凹槽内。墓葬中人骨已朽，部分可见残痕，显示墓主头向朝南。7座墓葬中，北排M5等级较低，墓葬尺寸较小。随葬品除陶器外，玉石器仅出土滑石串珠1组和石镰1件。总体而言，南排墓葬墓大坑深，级别较高。但南排M6情形比较特殊，其墓长达3.65、宽1.9米，体量宏大，现场判断其主体部分未遭后期扰动，但该墓随葬玉器较少，仅在头端和腹部位置分别发现玉璧、玉镯的残片，脚端陶器附近，有半成品玉镰及玉珠、玉锥形器各1件，似与其规模颇不相符。它是本次发掘的南排墓葬最东面的一座，但据调查，其东部早年曾

有一座出玉璧等玉器的高等墓葬被破坏,所以原先的南排贵族墓葬中,各墓位置的排列可能并不与随葬品所体现的级别产生对应关系。

　　姚家山墓葬内出土大量玉、石、陶、牙骨等珍贵文物,其中玉石器占大多数,其中有琮5件、三叉形器3件、钺4件、梳背3件、璧6件,以及镯、锥形饰、玉串饰、柱形器等,除以上所列良渚文化大墓中常见的器形外,还发现2件玉刀(“耕田器”),其中一件的顶部有冠状凸起。另外还出土5件玉镰,其中M1出土的一把玉镰的尾端亦有冠状凸,显示出较高的级别。此为这两类玉器在正式考古发掘中的首次发现。石器器形主要为厚体石钺,也有少量石镰、石镞等。M3就出土各类大小不一的厚体石钺25件,其中最大的一件高达33、宽为22厘米。另一件厚体石钺端部发现刻划图案,似为一人呈躬身状,颇为罕见。以往良渚文化大墓中极难保存的牙骨器在这批墓葬中保存相对较好,M2中出土的柄形象牙器上,运用剔地浅浮雕和阴线刻方式雕刻了精致的兽面纹,M3玉梳的象牙梳齿亦清晰可辨。另外,部分墓葬中还发现了漆器痕

玉琮
Jade *cone*

M7
Tomb M7

玉琮式管
Jade *cone*-shaped Tube

玉三叉形器（正面）
Three-pronged Jade Plaque (front)

玉三叉形器（背面）
Three-pronged Jade Plaque (back)

玉钺
Jade *yue*-ax

玉钺
Jade *yue*-ax

玉璧
Jade *bi*-disk

玉环
Jade *huan*-ring

刻纹石钺
Incised Stone *yue*-ax

彩绘石钺
Stone *yue*-ax Painted with Color

玉梳背
Jade Comb Base

玉镰
Jade Sickle

半成品玉镰
Half-finished Jade Sickle

M3 出土石钺
Stone *yue*-axes

玉 "耘田器"
Jade "Weeding Tool"

陶带甑鼎
Pottery *ding*-tripod with *zeng*-steamer

迹。墓葬的陶器数量较少，组合为带甑鼎、豆（或簋）、罐、盆，另有尊、双鼻壶等。其中 M2 的一件黑皮陶器盖上刻划数组鸟纹与龙蛇纹的精致图案。由陶鼎看，北排两墓随葬大敞口凹足鼎，形制独特，在以往发掘的良渚文化墓葬中少见。南排墓则多随葬鱼鳍足鼎。总体而言，这批墓葬大体属于良渚文化的中晚期，各墓的年代有早晚差异。

墓葬周围和土台的西部共发现 21 个长方形的土坑，皆与墓葬开口同一层。这些坑与土台走向平行而与墓葬保持垂直，长 1～1.8、宽 0.5～0.8、深 0.35～1 米，边壁陡直，平底或浅圈底，坑内填土纯净，基本不见包含物，少部分底部有黄白色细淤土面，显示坑内可能有过空间。根据以往对本地区其他地点类似迹象的分析，我们认为这些坑是与高台墓地或墓葬相关的祭祀坑。祭祀坑的分布似乎有一定规律，有的墓葬周围分布有多个，有的墓周围则没有。未发现墓葬打破祭祀坑的现象，而祭祀坑打破墓葬现象则有数例，甚至有的打断了墓底的棺椁线的痕迹，但没有发现坑打进墓葬中心位置的现象，说明一部分坑应与特定墓葬存在对应关系，开挖各该祭坑举行某种祭祀活动的时间与墓葬的埋设时间存在一定的间隔，推测可能是封土等地面标志模糊后无法确认墓葬的精确位置，使祭祀坑打入葬具位置。另外一些坑在位置上与墓葬相隔较远，可能与整个高台墓地相关。

姚家山是浙北地区近年来发现的最高级别的良渚文化墓地。桐乡、海宁一带是浙江余杭良渚遗址群外良渚文化遗址的另一个密集分布区域，姚家山的发掘为我们研究和探索良渚文化的区域类型、丧葬习俗、高土台的营建目的与过程、祭祀坑与墓葬的关系等诸多问题提供了重要线索和材料。

（供稿：王宁远 周伟民 朱宏中）

Yaojiashan is the location of the highest ranking cemetery of the Liangzhu Culture that has been recently identified in northern Zhejiang Province, and is also the center of multiple Liangzhu sites distributed in the areas of Tongxiang County and Haining County. From November 2004 to January 2005, the Zhejiang Provincial Institute of Archaeology launched rescue excavations on the site, exposing a total size of 1,300 sq m. The exposed Liangzhu features include an artificially built high platform cemetery, seven high ranking aristocratic tombs, and 21 sacrificial pits. The unearthed Liangzhu artifacts include more than 260 pieces (or sets) of pottery, jade, stone, ivory, and bone implements. The important achievements from the excavation provide invaluable clues and data for the study of various aspects of the Liangzhu Culture, including regional patterns, mortuary customs, the purpose and process of building high platforms as well as the relationship between sacrificial pits and tombs.

刻纹黑皮陶器盖
Incised Black Pottery Vessel Lid

江苏邳州
梁王城遗址发掘

**EXCAVATION OF THE LIANGWANGCHENG SITE
IN PIZHOU, JIANGSU**

梁王城遗址位于江苏省邳州市的北部，距市区37公里，隶属戴庄镇李圩村。遗址上现保存有高出周围农田1～2米的城墙，平面近长方形。南、北城墙保存较好，南城墙现残长900多米，北城墙残长800多米，南北城墙相距约1100米，遗址总面积100多万平方米。在遗址西部俗称的"金銮殿"高台的地表及河岸断崖发现有大量的扁凿形鼎足、鬲足、罐口沿、豆柄、板瓦、筒瓦等陶片，从断面观察文化层厚度达5米多。1957年，南京博物院考古调查发现该遗址，认为上部是汉到春秋战国时期的堆积，下部是商周时期的堆积。

2004年4月～2005年4月，由南京博物院考古研究所、徐州博物馆、邳州博物馆、南京大学考古专业共同组成的梁王城考古队对梁王城遗址进行了首次主动科学发掘，发掘总面积约1100平方米。发掘结果表明，遗址地层堆积从早到晚依次为大汶口文化层、龙山文化层、商周文化层、春秋战国文化层、北朝—隋文化层以及宋元文化层等。发现了大

汶口文化晚期的房址6座、儿童陶棺葬6座，龙山文化时期的浅地穴房址1座、墓葬1座，周代墓葬14座，春秋战国时期的大型夯土台基1处、北朝—隋时期的大型石础建筑基址1处，发现各个时期的遗迹计灰坑122座、灰沟6条、井5口、道路3条等，出土陶器、瓷器、石器、青铜器、玉器、骨器及琉璃器、铁盔甲、兵器、铁工具农具等共1000多件。另外，通过对南城墙的解剖和东、西、北城墙的调查钻探确定了梁王城城址的始建年代为战国时期，面积为100多万平方米。

现将发掘的主要收获介绍如下：

史前时期主要遗存包括大汶口文化时期和龙山文化时期的遗存。有房址、道路、灰坑、墓葬等。

在大汶口文化地层中共发现陶棺葬6座，以M6和M7保存较好。M6为长方形土坑竖穴墓，墓口长1、宽0.5、深0.35米，埋葬一儿童，以陶鼎作为葬具。陶鼎系打成大块的陶片，在墓底以鼎口沿、腹片相叠并排铺垫一层，然后把儿童放置其

大汶口文化 M6、M7
Tombs M6 and M7 of
the Dawenkou Culture

龙山文化 M20
Tomb M20 of the Longshan Culture

龙山文化 M20 玉玦出土情况
Exposed Jade *jue*-slit Ring at Tomb
M20 of the Longshan Culture

上，再以打碎的陶片盖满全身。人骨侧身，下肢稍弯曲，经鉴定其年龄在5岁左右。随葬有一件小器盖。葬具经拼对、复原，为2件器物，一件为折沿敞口深腹扁凿形足鼎，另一件为折沿敞口球形腹扁凿形足鼎。M7，为长方形土坑竖穴墓，墓口长1.5、宽0.55~0.6、深0.4米，北距M6约0.5米。埋葬一儿童，亦以陶鼎作为葬具。葬法与M6基本相同，随葬有一件喇叭形口鼓肩壶、一件杯形圈足尊、一件浅盘喇叭形圈足豆等器物，于墓主的盆骨前方发现一个狗的下颌骨。另外在墓主的颈部发现有2件玉管，应是墓主生前戴在项上的饰品。

龙山文化时期的主要遗迹有墓葬和房址等。M20为土坑竖穴墓，平面为圆角长方形，墓口

龙山文化F7人骨叠压及器物出土情况
Piled Human Bones and Associated Artifacts at House F7 of the Longshan Culture

龙山文化F7部分出土器物
Portion of the Unearthed Artifacts from House F7 of the Longshan Culture

长1.7、宽0.2~0.3、深0.25米。墓内埋葬一成年女性,俯身直肢,两手置于腹前,下肢交叉。在头骨两侧的耳部分别发现一件玉玦。

F7为1座浅地穴房址,平面呈圆角长方形,东西长4.55、南北宽2.6、深0.25米,门道朝南。共发现柱洞9个,由2个中心柱及7个边柱组成。在房内发现了6具非正常死亡的人骨及一个头骨,多有挣扎和叠压现象。经现场初步鉴定,1号、2号、5号人骨为壮年女性,3号、4号人骨为青年女性,7号人骨为少年女性,6号人骨为少年个体,性别不明。房址内的死者均为女性和未成年人,推测很可能是部落间的冲突导致了这场灾难。在房址的西南部有两大堆炊食器,多数比较完整,其中一堆陶

器有罐形矮足鼎、折沿鼓腹罐、觯形杯、单把罐、平底罐、卷沿盆各1件,覆碗形器盖3件;另一堆陶器有鸟喙形足鼎2件、折沿鼓腹平底罐3件、觯形杯2件、铲形足鼎、宽扁形足鼎、带流罐、覆碗形器盖、陶匣、双耳盆各1件。其中一件鸟喙形足大陶鼎内盛放着一件带流罐、一件折沿鼓腹平底罐、两件觯形杯等4件小器物。出土陶器组合较完整,时代特征明显,为龙山文化早期的典型器物。

历史时期的文化堆积和遗迹遗物也非常丰富,为解开梁王城之谜,对残存地表的城墙进行了解剖。在遗址的南城墙中部偏西布了一条正南北的探沟,规格为47×3米。发掘结果显示城墙主体底部宽约25、顶部现宽约12、高度现存约3米。城墙修

筑时，先将地面整平，挖两条相距3.2米的顺着墙体方向的宽基槽，接着填土夯实，然后在上面修筑墙体。运用版筑法层层夯筑，每层夯土厚约0.15米，现存夯层20层。夯窝十分明显，可分为两种，一种呈浅圆柱状，直径约6厘米，使用的是平头夯具，另一种呈圜底状，直径约5厘米，使用的是尖圆头夯具。据发掘及钻探的结果显示，在南城墙体的南面15米处有护城河，护城河宽约50米。在城墙的夯土里出土有较多的陶片及部分原始瓷片，有锥状绳纹鬲足、绳纹鬲卷口沿、小高领直口厚唇罐口沿、折腹豆盘、豆直柄、内底有水波纹的原始瓷片等，另有较多的印纹硬陶，纹饰有席纹、细小方格纹、方格内填"×"纹、小方格内填"米"字纹、"回"字形方格内填"×"纹等。在城墙主体下的灰坑里亦出有相类似的陶片。总之，出土陶片单纯，时代特征明显，表明城墙的建筑年代当在春秋战国之际。此外，我们在T7和T9的南部发现有东西长13多米、厚约0.7米的夯土台基，从层位关系及台基的包含物分析，该夯土台基属于春秋战国时期。虽然目前在探方里刚露了一小部分，但是为下一步的工作重点指明了方向，为解决梁王城城址的布局和性质提供了重要线索。

在北朝—隋时期的地层中发现一座大型石础建筑基址，编号为F5，现存11个石柱础。从已揭露的情况看，平面呈长方形，东西总长11.5、南北总宽8.2米。石柱础分为南北平行并排的3列，每列4个，中列西数第二个石柱础被一后期灰坑打掉。从目前清理的状况分析，F5尚向探方的西边和南边延伸。根据层位关系及各柱坑内出土的绳纹瓦片、青瓷片初步断定，F5的年代为北朝—隋时期。

总之，梁王城遗址史前时期堆积非常丰富，其大汶口文化龙山文化遗存与其附近的刘林遗址、大墩子遗址、花厅遗址共同构成黄淮地区史前文化圈，相互之间有着密切的关系。属于龙山文化早期的F7的房址内，发现了7具非正常死亡的人骨，不似居室葬，也没有发现洪水、火灾或是房屋倒塌等现象，屋内生活用的陶器完整放置于门道旁，所有骨骸都作挣扎状，并且几乎全部是妇女和未成年人，据此推测他们罹难于部落间的冲突，此类遗迹在龙山文化中尚属首次发现。

本次发掘确定梁王城为面积逾100万平方米，为战国时期苏北最大的城址，梁王城连同周围同时期的鹅鸭城遗址、九女墩墓地共同构成了黄淮地区

龙山文化F7部分出土器物
Portion of the Unearthed Artifacts
from House F7 of the Longshan Culture

周代陶鬲（G4：8）
Pottery *li*-tripod of
the Zhou Period (G4：8)

周代陶鬲（H81：1）
Pottery *li*-tripod of the Zhou Period (H81：1)

梁王城南城墙解剖现场
Cross-section Trenching
on the Southern Wall

春秋战国时期的历史框架。北朝—隋时期的大型石础建筑基址和诸多遗物的发现对研究南北朝时期的历史文化也具有极高的价值。

（供稿：周润垦 张浩林 原丰）

南城墙夯窝揭露情况
Hollow Signs of Clay Pounding on the Southern Wall

北朝-隋时期大型石础建筑（F5）
Large Stone-based Structure of the Northern
Dynasties – Sui Dynasty Period

T7、T9发掘现场
Excavation in Test Squares T7 and T9

From April 2004 to April 2005, archaeologists from the Institute of Archaeology of the Museum of Nanjing and several other archaeological units in Jiangsu Province carried out the first excavations at the Liangwangcheng walled site, exposing a total area of around 1,100 sq m. The results of the excavations indicate that the deposit layers of the site belong to, in chronological order, the Dawenkou Culture, the Longshan Culture, the Shang - Zhou period, the Eastern Zhou period, the Northern Dynasties - Sui dynasty, and the Song - Yuan period.

The major identified features from the site include six house foundations and six child urn-coffins of the late Dawenkou Culture, one shallow subterranean house foundation and one burial of the Longshan Culture, 14 burials of the Zhou period, one large rammed earth platform of the Spring and Autumn period, and one large stone-based architecture foundation of the Northern Dynasties - Sui dynasty. The over 1,000 artifacts unearthed from the site belong to various types, including pottery, porcelain, stone implements, bronze vessels, jades, bone implements, glass wares, iron armor and helmet, and other iron weapons and agricultural tools.

In addition, it was verified through trenching on the southern wall and auger drilling on the other three sides, that the walls were initially built in the Warring States period, and the size of the walled site spread more than 1,000,000 sq m. In the Huang-Huai region (where the Yellow River and the Huaihe River branch), the walled Liangwangcheng site is associated with contemporary neighboring sites such as the Eyacheng walled site and the Jiunudun cemetery, together shaping the regional history of the Eastern Zhou period; the Dawenkou and Longshan remains of the Liangwangcheng site are an integral component of our knowledge of the cultural sphere of the earlier Neolithic period, as are other neighboring Neolithic sites at Liulin, Dadunzi, and Huating. Therefore, the Liangwangcheng site is important for the study of prehistoric settlement patterns and the process of ancient civilization in the Huang-Huai region.

河南鹤壁刘庄遗址

THE LIUZHUANG SITE IN HEBI, HENAN

刘庄遗址位于河南省鹤壁市淇滨区大赉店镇刘庄村南，为市级文物保护单位，西北与著名的辛村墓地相邻、东南1.5公里为大赉店遗址。1932年，原中央研究院历史语言研究所郭宝均先生等在发掘辛村墓地期间调查发现该遗址。遗址面积30余万平方米，文化堆积厚0.6~1.5米。

作为南水北调中线工程首批实施的文物保护控制性项目之一，经报请国家文物局批准，2005年7~9月河南省文物考古研究所会同鹤壁市文物工作队，邀请郑州大学、山东大学师生40余人组成考古队伍对遗址进行了考古勘探和发掘。10~12月，河南省文物考古研究所再次进行发掘。在遗址东部共布10×10米探方76个、5×10米探方2个，发掘面积7700平方米，发现大批仰韶文化晚期大司空类型遗迹、遗物以及较大规模的下七垣文化墓地。

大司空类型文化遗存发现窖穴和灰坑436座、房基1座、陶窑1座、灰土堆积9个、陶片铺垫遗迹5个、灰沟9条以及大批居址柱洞。

房基F1仅残存南北向基槽，可推知为地面式长方形房基，木骨泥墙。房址柱洞主要分布在发掘区中北部和西部，圆形袋状窖穴多成片分布在其周围，由此可知发掘区北部、西部应为居址区域。

灰坑有圆形、椭圆形、不规则形口几种，多为浅坑。灰沟均为西北一东南走向，有的可能与居址分布有关。HG6长约75、宽0.9米左右，贯穿伸出发掘区域，沟底人工铺垫石块，下为碎石子和砂粒，其北高南低，高差约40厘米，结合遗址地貌

遗址发掘探方布方情况
Allocation of Test Squares on the Site

新时器时代居址柱洞分布
Distribution of Postholes in Neolithic Residential Site

新时器时代灰坑中石块堆积
Rubble Filled in Neolithic Pit

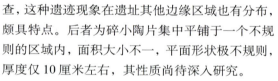

新时器时代灰沟 HG6
Neolithic Ditch HG6

分析该灰沟可能具有排水功用。

　　发掘所见灰土堆积和陶片铺垫遗迹现象值得注意，前者类似以往所称不规则形灰坑，分布面积少则近百平方米、多则几百平方米，横跨五六个探方，一般较浅，底部坑洼不平，有的直接坐落在砾石层上，包含物远较一般窖穴、灰坑丰富。通过调

查，这种遗迹现象在遗址其他边缘区域也有分布，颇具特点。后者为碎小陶片集中平铺于一个不规则的区域内，面积大小不一，平面形状极不规则，厚度仅 10 厘米左右，其性质尚待深入研究。

　　出土遗物主要为陶、石、鹿角器等。夹砂陶略多于泥质陶，有灰陶、褐陶、红陶等。陶器以素面

新时器时代夹砂陶罐
Neolithic Coarse Pottery *guan*-jar

新时器时代彩陶罐残片
Neolithic Painted Pot Pieces

墓地东、西区相交部位
Connecting Area between
Eastern and Western Dis-
tricts

M145 石棺墓及其周围墓葬分
布情况
Stone-coffin Tomb M145
and Neighboring Graves

为主，纹饰有附加堆纹、篮纹、弦纹、划纹、席纹、压印纹等，其中以附加堆纹最多，腹部装饰鸡冠耳、口部压印花边作风较为流行。彩陶数量不多，均红彩、黑彩，纹样有弧边三角纹、斜线纹、竖线纹、同心圆纹、水波纹、平行条带纹、睫毛纹等，饰于泥质罐、盆、钵、碗等器。器类不甚丰富，夹砂陶器以素面罐最为常见，还有小罐、篮纹罐、盆、瓮、器盖等；泥质陶器有小口高领壶、折腹盆、罐、钵、碗、纺轮等，陶环数量较多。石器有大型石铲、斧、凿、锛、钻头、环、纺轮等。鹿角器见有角铲。骨器、蚌器极少，出土兽骨数量少，水生动物遗骸

基本不见。

上述文化遗存和分布于豫北冀南地区的大司空类型面貌特征相近，当属大司空类型文化遗存。

下七垣文化墓地基本完整揭露，发现墓葬336座，出土器物近500件。

墓地大致分布于东西110、南北55米的范围内，在空间上分为东、南、西三块，三者相连布局呈"U"字形。以墓葬朝向为标准，可将其分为东、西两大区。东区墓葬多头向东，南北成行排列，西区墓葬多头向北、东西成行排列。各区均由若干排墓葬组成，少者七八排，多者十余排，排列较为规律。从

M10全景
Comprehensive View of Tomb M10

M14全景
Comprehensive View of Tomb M14

M10陶器组合
Composition of Pottery Wares in Tomb M10

M24出土陶鬲
Pottery li-tripod Unearthed from Tomb M24

墓区规模、墓葬数量上观察，西Ⅱ区规模最大，分布墓葬181座，西Ⅰ区、东区递次，东区分布墓葬不到60座。相对而言，东区墓葬分布稍显稀疏，西区墓葬排列较为密集。有趣的是东区、西Ⅰ区之间有一排东向墓将二者连接，使两者之间无法明确分界，这种排列布局原因何在值得探讨。

墓葬多为长方形竖穴土坑墓，个别口部为长椭

圆形，一般较为狭长，大小稍有差别。墓葬均为单人葬，葬式仰身直肢或俯身直肢，骨架保存一般较差，有的甚至仅见几颗牙齿。多数墓葬不见葬具，有的有木质单棺，有的在墓底残存近长方形的纯净黑土痕迹，与墓葬填土明显不同，不排除为垫尸木板或其他铺垫物的可能。M145为石棺墓，墓口长2.61、宽0.65米，石棺由13块自然片石组成，长

M185 木棺痕迹
Traces of Remains of Wooden Coffin in Tomb M185

M94 随葬陶鬲
Pottery li-tripod Buried in Tomb M94

2.25米、宽0.45~0.5米，上部平盖三块片石，墓底未见石块。墓主俯身直肢，骨骼粗壮，应为男性，墓主脚部随葬陶鬲1件。另外，还有近20座墓葬在墓主头脚两端各放置一块或多块石头。

有随葬品的墓葬208座，占墓葬总数的60%以上，一般随葬陶器1~6件不等，大多放置在墓主脚部、头端。随葬陶器以夹砂灰陶居多，次为泥质灰陶，有一定数量的泥质褐胎灰皮或黑皮陶。陶器纹饰以绳纹为主，有凸弦纹、凹弦纹、绳切纹、压印圆涡纹等，有圆形和"工"字形镂孔。器类有鬲、罐、鼎、豆、圈足盘、盆、簋、鬶、爵、甗、尊、斝、器盖等，以鬲、罐、豆、盆、圈足盘最为常见。陶器组合差异明显，有近40种组合之多，其中随葬单件陶鬲的墓葬最多，次为随葬单件夹砂罐的，其他稍多见的组合还有鬲、豆，鬲、盆，鬲、豆、盆，鬲、豆、圈足盘，罐、豆、簋等。少数墓葬随葬有石钺、绿松石串饰等。M35出土的齿刃石钺加工精良，整体为横向长方形，与二里头遗址竖向长方形、两侧装饰扉棱的玉钺（戚）不同。值得注意的是，东区随葬陶器中鬲均为肥袋足鬲、多夹砂罐，西区则大多为卷沿鼓腹鬲、夹砂罐少，而且东区墓葬随葬品数量往往较少，两者墓葬主流朝向不同，其成因尚有待深入研究。

关于墓地年代的上下限，我们根据随葬陶鬲的形态特征可做初步推测：M94：1陶鬲为薄胎、高领、肥乳袋足，腹饰绳纹至实足根，表现了较早的特点，与河北徐水巩固庄采集：1鬲有近似之处。M24：1陶鬲侈口、卷沿、鼓腹，方唇微上折，与二里岗下层C1H9陶鬲接近，年代亦应差距不大。从墓葬出土陶器特征观察，鬲、鼎、深腹罐、豆、盆、甗、器盖等与下七垣文化同类陶器特征近同，圈足盘以往较为少见，应同当地龙山文化有一定关联。而肥袋足鬲、鬶、爵、斝等陶器则反映了以卷沿鼓腹鬲为主体特征的下七垣文化在发展进程中融合、吸取周边地区多元文化因素的特点。

在中原地区，如此规模的夏时代的公共墓地属首次发现，为先商文化的发掘研究工作填补了一项空白。尽管高规格墓葬未有发现，但墓地布局清楚、保存完整、随葬品较为丰富，是研究其墓葬制度、社会结构、商人渊源、夏商关系等学术问题的重要实物资料。

（供稿：赵新平 韩朝会）

To mitigate the impact caused by the Middle Route Project of the South-to-north Water Diversion, archaeologists mainly from the Henan Provincial Institute of Archaeology carried out excavations at the Liuzhuang site in Hebi City, Henan Province from July to December 2005. A total area of 7,700 sq m was exposed during the excavation, and the strata of the deposit were primarily formed in two cultural periods. The deposit of lower layers is dated to the late Yangshao Culture, and the exposure of the settlement of the Dasikongcun Type of the Yangshao Culture is helpful for the further study of this archaeological culture type and related issues. From the upper layers of the site dated to the Xia period, a cemetery of the Xiaqiyuan Culture was fully unearthed, within which 336 graves were regularly arranged. The discovery of a cemetery under controlled management fulfills a blank in the study of pre-Shang culture. The stone coffins and simplified grave structures are also a first-time discovery in the Central Plains of the Xia period, providing new threads of the origin of the Shang clan to explore.

M218随葬器物组合
Composition of Pottery Wares Buried in Tomb M218

河北唐县北放水遗址

THE BEIFANGSHUI SITE IN TANGXIAN, HEBEI

北放水遗址位于保定市唐县高昌镇北放水村西北台地，台地中部被一冲沟阻断，地理单元属太行山东麓丘陵与平原混合地带。遗址面积约110000平方米，其中在南水北调渠线内面积约40000平方米。该遗址是河北省配合南水北调工程首批开展工作的控制性项目之一，规划发掘面积5600平方米，本年度发掘面积3100平方米。

河北省文物研究所会同保定市文物管理所、唐县文物保管所组成联合考古队，2005年4～12月对遗址进行考古发掘。共布5×5米探方119个，共计发现各类灰坑288个、半地穴式房址3座、灰沟15条、竖穴土坑墓3座、瓮棺1座。出土陶、石器残件近35000件，其中可复原陶器50余件，小件标本200余件（其中石器140件）。陶器器类有鬲、瓶、盆、罐、豆、瓮、釜等，石器有穿孔刀、镰、斧、铲等，另发现环首小铜刀、铜镞、穿孔玉饰件和骨簪等，时代包括夏、东周及西汉三个时期，其中以夏时期遗存最为重要。

西汉时期遗迹发现一处素面青砖砌就的长方形简易建筑址，内填充不规则形条石块及板瓦、筒瓦、敞口卷沿鼓腹罐等残件。东周时期遗迹有灰坑、灰沟和土坑墓、瓮棺，灰坑为平面近圆形或不规则形斜壁圜底状；灰沟多为自然冲沟，平面形状不规则，宽窄不一，斜壁，圜底；土坑墓为竖穴长条形，无葬具、无随葬品，人骨为仰身直肢，保存极差；瓮棺为夹蚌红陶釜对接，未发现人骨。

夏时期遗迹以形态各异的灰坑为主。依平面形状可分为圆形、近圆形、椭圆形、长方形、不规则形等五类，结构为斜壁、直壁、袋状以及平底、圜底、不规则形底等，多为人工挖掘以倾倒废弃物或利用自然坑穴堆积遗弃物。

H13平面呈椭圆形，直壁，经人工修整，圜底。填土为灰黑土，疏松，掺杂大量红烧土块。坑底也堆积大量红烧土块，皆为草拌泥块，大小不一，大者长约0.20米、小者仅长约0.05米，部分土块烧结程度高，呈青灰色，泥块上可见规整的转角，表面草秸痕明显。出土有夹云母灰陶、夹云母黑皮红陶、夹云母红陶、夹砂灰陶及泥质灰陶等器物残

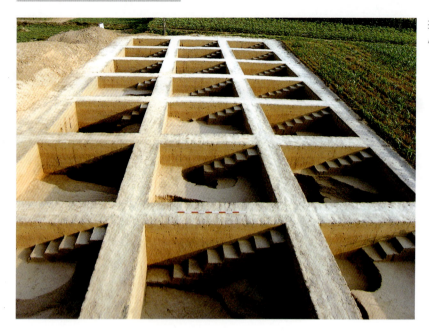

探方布置情况
Allocation of Test Squares

片，可辨器形有鬲残片、甗腰、瓮口沿、瓮圈足、折腹盆残片等。

房址皆为简陋的近圆形半地穴式，直壁或斜坡状壁，活动面为略经踩实的生土硬面，较平或中部略凹，局部有不规则烧土硬面，环壁一周发现有大小不一的柱洞底残迹，门道开向南或东，其中一座房址在近门道处发现有近圆形土坑灶。

出土遗物中西汉时期有绳纹板瓦、筒瓦及卷沿灰陶盆等。东周时期遗物有夹蚌灰陶折沿方唇乳突状足根粗绳纹鬲、泥质灰陶细柄碗形豆及夹蚌红陶敞口沿上翘长腹圜底釜及三棱状小铜镞、弧刃拱背环首小铜刀。夏时期遗物以陶、石器为主，另有小型玉器、骨器等。陶器陶质有夹云母黑皮红陶、灰陶，夹砂黑皮红陶，夹砂灰陶、红陶，泥质红陶、灰陶及泥质磨光黑陶等。器类有卷沿高领袋足鬲、饰附加堆纹甗腰、鼓腹罐、弧腹罐、弧腹盆、折腹盆、敛口蛋形圈足瓮、敛口折肩平底瓮、深腹豆及纺轮等，以侈口卷沿高领鬲、长颈袋足鬲和敛口内勾蛋形圈足瓮最富特征，纹饰有细绳纹、中绳纹、弦断绳纹、索链状附加堆纹、细线刻划纹、楔形戳印纹、压印圆涡纹等，小件陶器有蘑菇状器纽、陀螺状纺轮、圆形陶片、弹丸等。石器种类有长条形穿孔石刀、弯月形石镰、亚腰形石铲、梯形石斧等。玉器为片状穿孔小饰

H3内填充的红烧土块和陶器残件
Burned Clayclods and Pottery Pieces in PitH13

T0503内遗迹分布情况
Feature Distributed in Test Square T0503

高领陶鬲
High Necked *li*—tripod

长颈陶鬲
Long Necked *li*—tripod

敛口蛋形圈足陶瓮
Egg-shaped *weng*—urn
on pedestal

敛口折肩陶瓮
weng—urn with Contracted
Mouth and Angular Body

弧腹陶盆
pen—basin with Curved Body

折腹陶盆
pen—basin with Angular Body

粗绳纹陶鬲
li—tripod with Coarse Cord Marks

红陶釜
Reddish Pottery *fu*—cauldron

梯形石斧
Stone Ax in Trapezoid Shape

亚腰形石铲
Stone Spade with Narrowed Waist

件，骨器为圆锥状残骨簪。

　　北放水遗址夏时期文化遗存的发现，是近年来保定地区田野考古的重要收获。以往对于此类遗存只进行过调查或小范围试掘，且多集中于保北地区，学者称之为"保北型"先商文化或"下岳

各庄"文化，其与豫北冀南发现的先商文化、晋中和北方等夏时期考古学文化既有联系，又有区别，有鲜明的地域特征，北放水遗址夏时期文化遗存的发现对廓清该地区夏时期考古学文化面貌有重要意义。

（供稿：徐海峰）

The Beifangshui site is situated on a terrace which lies northwest of Beifangshui village in Gaochang, Tangxian County, Hebei Province. Topographically, the site is surrounded by alternating hills and plains at the eastern foot of the Taihang Mountains.

As a rescue program for the Middle Route Project of the South-to-North Water Diversion, archaeologists from the Hebei Provincial Institute of Cultural Relics excavated the Beifangshui site from April to December in 2005. During the field season, 119 test squares each measuring 5 m by 5 m were allocated and a total area of 3,100 sq m was actually exposed. Numerous features were identified, including 288 pits in various shapes, three semi-subterranean house foundations, 15 ditches, three vertical pit burials, and one urn coffin. Nearly 35,000 lithic and pottery artifacts were unearthed, including more than 50 restorable wares and over 200 special findings. The majority of the artifacts were dated to the Xia period and the rest to the Eastern Zhou or the Western Han.

The exposed features from the site are mainly pits and ditches in either round or irregular shapes. Among the unearthed artifacts, pottery wares were the largest category and stone implements the second. Two pottery types are most distinctive: one is the *li*-tripod with bag-shaped legs and a rolled rim, and the other is the egg-shaped *weng*-urn on a pedestal. The lithic types include bored knife, curved sickle, narrow-waisted spade, and trapezoid ax.

The Beifangshui site has the first identified Xia remains south of the Baoding district. Archaeological remains from the site only indicate associations with the contemporaneous pre-Shang Culture in northern Henan and southern Hebei, with the Xia-period Culture in central Shanxi, and with the Xiajiadian Lower-stratum Culture to the north, but also present obvious regional characteristics. The discoveries from the Beifangshui site therefore are important for the study of archaeological cultures of the Xia period with regard to aspects of cultural appearance, nature, distribution and interaction.

河北邯郸陈岩嵛遗址

THE CHENYANYU SITE IN HANDAN, HEBEI

为配合青（岛）红（其拉甫）高速公路冀鲁界至邯郸段建设工程，由河北省文物研究所、邯郸市文物研究所、邯郸县文物保管所联合组成考古队，2005年6~8月对邯郸县陈岩嵛遗址进行了发掘。

陈岩嵛遗址位于邯郸县户村镇陈岩嵛村西约300米，地势平坦。本次共发掘5×5米探方40个，并对重要遗迹进行适当扩方，发掘面积总计1010平方米。清理房址2座、灰坑41个、灰沟4条、墓葬2座。出土陶器、卜甲、卜骨、石器、骨器、蚌器、铜器共计180余件。

陈岩嵛遗址地层堆积共分5层，以晚商文化遗存为主，并有周代文化层和魏晋时期墓葬。

陈岩嵛遗址发现的遗迹主要有房址、灰坑、墓葬等。

房址2座，分为圆角长方形和圆形两类。

T0610④下F1为圆角长方形，方向为285°，东西长约4.5、南北宽约3.8~4.1、残高1米，北部发现灶一个，门道位于西南，为台阶式斜坡门道，残长1.6、宽0.6、台高0.15米，四壁均有不同程度的坍塌，居住面较平整。

T0918④下F2为圆形，方向131°，直径2.3、残深0.5米，斜坡形门道残长0.5、宽0.6米，共发现前后两个柱洞。

灰坑41个，分为圆形、椭圆形、不规则形三类。其中圆形灰坑25个、椭圆形灰坑12个、不规则形灰坑4个。其中H7为晚商灰坑，形状为圆形、直壁、平底，直径1.4、深1米，底部有完整狗骨架一具，填土中发现残刻辞卜甲，文字只残存半个，推测为晚商祭祀遗迹。

墓葬2座，M1为魏晋时期的砖室墓，M2为瓦棺墓，打破第三层西周层。在M2外有西周文化层及灰坑。墓向为117°，长1.2、宽0.5、残深0.5米。M2为仰身直肢葬，骨架上覆盖一层器物残片，主要有罐底等大块残片，下层铺垫一层器物残片。

此次对陈岩嵛遗址的发掘，清理的文化层及遗迹以商代为主，出土遗物以陶器为主，另有大量石器、骨器及少量卜骨、卜甲、蚌器、角器和贝饰。

陶器以夹砂灰陶和泥质灰陶为主，还有夹砂红陶和泥质红陶、夹砂褐陶、泥质褐陶、夹粗砂灰陶、夹粗砂红陶，另有少量磨光灰陶和磨光褐陶。纹饰以中绳纹、粗绳纹为主，另有少量细绳纹、弦断绳纹、交错绳纹、交错弦断绳纹、弦纹、素面、附加堆纹、菱形纹、方格纹等。遗址中出土大量陶器，但可复原陶器的较少，可辨器形以罐、鬲、豆为主，另有盆、瓮、簋、甑、碗、纺轮、网坠及圆形陶片等。

F1
House Feature F1

F2 及周围灰坑
House Feature F2
and Neighboring Pits

H7 祭祀坑
Ritual Pit H7

出土的石器有斧、铲、刀、镰、镞、纺轮、网坠及圆形石片。骨器则有刀、铲、锯、簪及骨料。此外还出土卜骨1件、卜甲9片以及蚌器、角器、贝饰等。

这次发掘所获古遗迹、遗物甚为丰富，文化遗存时代包括商代、西周、魏晋、宋，其中以商代遗存为主，出土的周代刻辞卜甲是此次发掘的重要收获。陈岩嵜遗址的发掘，为冀南地区商代文化研究提供了重要的考古学资料。

（供搞：高建强）

蚌锯
Shell Saw

角锥
Antler Awl

卜骨、卜甲
Oracle Bone and
Oracle Turtle Shell

陶簋
Pottery gui—Container

The Chenyanyu site is located in a plain area around 300 m west of Chenyanyu village in Hucun, Handan County, Hebei Province. The field work in 2005 excavated an area of 1,010 sq m allocated with 40 test squares each measuring 5 m by 5 m. A variety of features were identified, including two house ruins, 41 pits, four ditches, and two burials. 181 artifacts were unearthed, including pottery wares, oracle turtle shells, oracle bones, implements made of stone, bone or shell, and bronze artifacts as well.

The deposit of the Chenyanyu site consists of five layers. Archaeological remains were mainly from the late Shang period, but cultural deposit of the Zhou period and tombs of the Wei - Jin period were also present.

Both the identified semi-subterranean house structures are dated to the Shang period. Orientated to 285 degrees (according to the direction of the doorway), House F1 has a rectangular shape with rounded corners, measuring 4.5 m from east to west and 3.8 - 4.1 m from north to south. The remaining subterranean structure is

around 1 m deep, and the four corners were more or less collapsed. The floor is relatively flat, and a fire hearth was found at the northeastern corner. The sloping doorway is situated in the southwest of the house, with a remaining length of 1.6 m and a width of 0.6 m.

The identified 41 pits are classified into three types based on the shape of the pit opening, namely round, oval and irregular. Of these pits, Pit H7 is most significant. It was round in opening, vertically cut, and leveled at the bottom. It measures 1.4 m in diameter and 1 m in depth. At the bottom of the pit a whole dog skeleton was found, and in the fill of the pit a piece of inscribed oracle bone was collected, which bears a remaining half of a character. Pit H7 is dated to the late Shang and is probably a sacrificial feature. The sacrificial pit and inscribed oracle bone are the important achievements of the 2005 excavation at the Chenyanyu site, and these discoveries provide important archaeological data for the study of the Shang Culture in the southern Hebei area.

新疆昆仑山
流水墓地考古发掘

ARCHAEOLOGICAL DISCOVERIES
AT THE LIUSHUI CEMETERY IN MT. KUNLUN, XINJIANG

流水墓地位于新疆和田地区于田县阿羌乡昆仑山深处流水村（现名喀什塔什）附近克里雅河上游河道与流水河交汇处的阿克布拉克台地。南距于田县城约100公里。

台地基本上属于相对狭长的平整缓坡，东西长131、南北最宽处35米，南面、东面俱为断崖，海拔高度2850米。

2002年7~8月，中国社会科学院考古研究所新疆队在昆仑山北麓考察古代玉石之路之际，于台地南部断崖边缘的出露墓葬，发现陶器与人骨。陶器形制与塔克拉玛干南部迄今所发现陶器虽有相似之处，但风格更为古朴，其独特的刻划纹饰，为以前所未见。对采集人骨所作的^{14}C测年结果为2950±50年。上述情况说明流水墓地很可能蕴含着昆仑山地区迄今发现最早的古代文化。

2003~2005年，中国社会科学院考古研究所新疆队连续三次系统全面地发掘了整个墓地，三年累计发掘52座墓葬，发掘面积约4000平方米。

墓葬均被掩埋在塔克拉玛干尘降形成的沙土之下，最厚的埋藏深度达4米。墓葬和地表之间的距离因地表坡度而异。最浅的墓葬石围顶部与地面之间相距0.66米，最深的4米。墓葬开口应该在石堆或石围之下0.2~1米不等。墓葬封堆上多散布有陶片。

根据卵石的排列和堆积的状况，可以将墓葬分为石堆墓与石围墓两种类型。卵石垂直堆积成椭圆形或圆角长方形，中间填充沙土和零星卵石的为石围墓；石堆墓大体由卵石覆盖成椭圆形，中间少有空缺。部分石堆或石围表面有焚烧的痕迹，有的石堆之中伴出故意砸碎的碎陶器。值得注意的是，近一半墓葬石堆或石围东部有一个小石圈相连，小石圈内多有用火痕迹。

墓室均为竖穴土坑，平面多呈椭圆形或圆角长方形。墓室大致为东西向，长1~2.2、宽0.6~2、深0.3~2.2米。填土多含有小砾石和零星的较大卵石；墓葬开口处常填有较大的扁平卵石，骨架上一般压有数块较大卵石。

绝大多数墓葬以多人合葬为主，多数骨架为二次葬。骨架被分层埋葬，常见一层或两层，部分墓葬的骨架为三层。一次性葬入的完整骨架各层均有，二次葬的骨架多堆置于墓室的西部。单人葬墓有8座、双人合葬墓有6座。葬式为仰身或侧身屈肢，接近人骨处陪葬有家畜头骨和四蹄，一般以山羊为主，个别规格较高的用马。

　　7座墓有尸床朽木的痕迹，尸床位于墓底，由2根纵向木棍和6根横向短木构成，尸床的四角都捆绑有竖立的木棍，横木搭或捆绑在纵向长木之上，并超出3～5厘米。尸床长1.4、宽0.8米。值得注意的是，7座保存有尸床痕迹的墓葬均为单个墓主。因填土较为湿润，入葬时人体是否有覆盖物已无从判断。

　　墓内的随葬品多寡不一，有的没有随葬品，多

石堆墓 M43
Rock-piled Tomb M43

石围墓 M35
Rock-surrounded
Tomb M35

多人葬
Multiple Burial

者陶器可达7件或铜刀4件，并伴有其他器物。

52座墓葬中出土陶器共80件、砺石8件、石眉笔12件，此外还有贝或蚌、金器和少量铁器。

陶器器形有罐、钵、杯、盆等，常见为罐钵组合。陶质以夹砂红陶为主，未见泥质红陶或灰陶。器物表面多有刻划纹饰，也有戳刺和压印纹。主要纹饰有三角纹、弦纹、菱纹、网纹和波纹等，偶见斜"目"字纹和麦穗纹。

铜器中最典型的是铜刀，共出26件。此外还有铜扣、铜珠、铜镞、铜马具、耳坠、手镯、铜镜等。

石器中最多见的是作为串饰的料珠，料珠的数量和类型较多。一座墓中常见数十枚，最多可至数百枚。其次为砺石，每座墓常见有1或2件砺石。长方形砺石较为多见，一端穿孔，另一端弧形内收，个别砺石为三角形。石眉笔与炭精块（画眉染料）也常见于墓葬之中。

玉器主要有玛瑙珠和玉佩。金器有耳坠、珠子和腰带等。骨角器有贝壳、蚌壳、骨珠，另有兽角马镳、骨镞以及发饰。铁器仅为数件残片，其中1件隐约可以看出铁刀的形状。

铜镜
Bronze Mirror

铜斧形器
Ax-shaped Bronze Implement

铜马衔
Bronze Horse Curb Bits

从墓葬形制和丧葬风格来看,流水墓葬与昆仑山以西巴基斯坦北部犍陀罗地区提马尔伽哈墓地文化为代表的"残肢葬"较为接近。

陶器器形与乌兹别克斯坦费尔干纳盆地的楚斯特文化的陶器如双耳罐、杯、钵等亦有接近之处。而陶器器形和纹饰均有相似之处的仅有西藏拉萨河谷曲贡墓地出土的个别单耳陶罐,新疆地区已有考古学文化中陶器纹饰类似的尚未发现,器形类似的诸如且末扎滚鲁克墓地等应是流水墓地陶器器形的后来继承者,年代差距较远。

铜刀风格与新疆察吾乎沟文化、哈密焉布拉克墓葬的类似,铃式耳坠与西伯利亚地区早期斯基泰文化中的耳环样式相似,铜质马镳、马衔、带尾钩箭镞亦与西伯利亚阿尔瓒(Arzan)出土器物相近。

综合上述情况,流水墓地所代表的考古学文化年代当在公元前1千纪前后。已经做出的 ^{14}C 测年数据与这一年代判断也较为接近。

发掘过程中,我们注意到石堆墓和石堆并非纯粹由卵石堆积而成,先是在石圈内堆土,之后在土堆上一圈圈覆盖卵石块。这种构建方式不是由于卵石来源不够或取运不方便,因为墓地所在台地临近的两条河道以及周边到处满布卵石。只能是距今3000年前后流水人的一种墓葬地表形式构筑理念。石围墓的石围圈数也并无一定之规,其中部上层大都有零星卵石块,因此石圈墓有可能最初就是石堆墓,石堆墓上部石块被后来的埋葬者取用,仅剩下底部的石圈。

大约有半数石堆或石围墓的东部都有一个直径约0.4~0.6米的小石圈,部分石圈内有火烧的痕迹。流水墓葬的方向基本上都向东,小石圈可能是作为一种墓向标志摆设在墓边,用火遗迹可能表示小石圈是火食祭祀活动的专属场地。

墓地居民对于死者的处理方式,最常见的是同一墓葬中一次葬与二次葬共用。一次性葬入的有多个个体与单个个体之分,单个个体应当是自然死亡,多个个体则很可能是死于瘟疫。战争死亡的可

陶双耳罐
Pottery *guan*-jar with
Double Handles

陶双耳罐
Pottery *guan*-jar with
Double Handles

陶单耳罐
Pottery *guan*-jar with
Single Handle

陶深腹罐
Pottery *guan*-jar with Deep Body

陶钵
Pottery *bo*-bowl

陶钵
Pottery *bo*-bowl

能性不大，因为人骨上没有暴力痕迹。集体埋葬中一次性入葬的个体很可能是当时社会某一群体中的重要人物，二次入葬的人骨则可能是先前死亡的一般性成员。

　　流水墓地是首次在昆仑山北麓发现的青铜时代墓葬，为昆仑山北麓地区迄今所发现年代最早的古代文化。流水墓地系统全面的考古发掘，取得了较为翔实的考古学资料，为探讨昆仑山地区距今3000年前后的文化面貌提供了可能，也为新疆地区史前时代考古学文化序列的确立提供了一定的帮助。

（供稿：巫新华 艾力江 艾再孜 喀斯穆）

The Liushui cemetery is located on a terrace deep in Mt. Kunlun at Liushui village in Aqiang, Yutian County, in the Xinjiang Uygur Autonomous Region. The excavation of the Liushui cemetery has revealed for the first time an ancient culture in Xinjiang which is characterized by a pure assemblage of incised pottery wares. During the period from 2003 to 2005, the Xinjiang Archaeological Team of the Institute of Archaeology of the Chinese Academy of Social Sciences, fully excavated the cemetery, exposing 52 burials in total. Two kinds of burial structures were found in the cemetery: one is piled up with rocks and the other surrounded using rocks. The characteristics of the unearthed artifacts are mainly represented by distinctive incised patterns on pottery wares, metal ornaments with the Scythian style as well as bronze knives, axes, spears and horse curb bits with a style that is different from that of the Central Plains and northern steppe. The cemetery has also yielded the earliest jade wares so far unearthed in Xinjiang and stone implements with Xinjiang regional characteristics. Dating to 3,000 BP, the Liushui cemetery is the first burial site of the Bronze Age discovered north of Mt. Kunlun, and is also evidence of the earliest ancient culture discovered north of Mt. Kunlun.

串饰
Beads

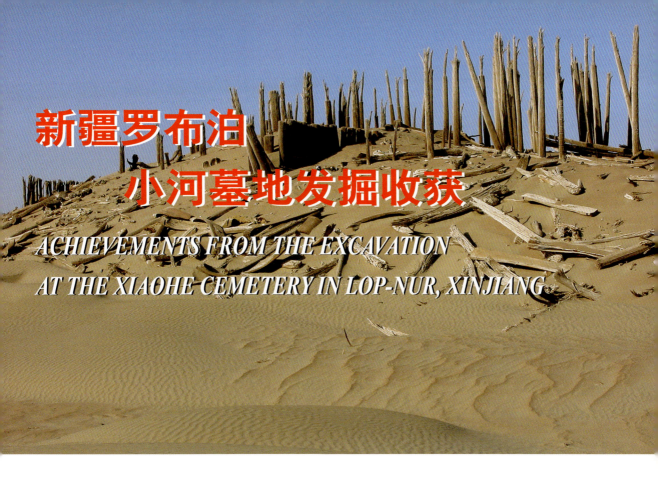

新疆罗布泊
小河墓地发掘收获

ACHIEVEMENTS FROM THE EXCAVATION
AT THE XIAOHE CEMETERY IN LOP-NUR, XINJIANG

位于罗布泊西南荒漠中的小河墓地，1934年瑞典考古学家贝格曼进行首次调查发掘，2002～2005年间，新疆文物考古研究所与吉林大学边疆考古研究中心合作，发掘墓葬167座，对整个墓地进行了全面的揭露，出土珍贵文物数以千计。

小河墓地处于孔雀河南部支流小河东侧约4公里处，外观为一个椭圆形沙山，发掘前测得其高度7米余，长74、宽35米左右。

墓地南部保存相对较好，墓葬可分五层，底层即第五层墓葬建构于原生沙丘上，这层墓葬形成之后，在其分布区的南北两侧各立一排整齐的木栅墙。南侧的木栅墙为墓地南边界墙，北木栅墙以北的区域，在木栅墙出现之后也开始布墓，此后整个墓地可分为南、北两个墓区。南墓区，在底层墓葬之上很快形成厚的风积沙层，墓葬由下而上层层有序叠埋，共分五层，计139座；北墓区由于罗布泊强烈的东北风的侵蚀，绝大部分墓葬都被破坏，特别是上层遗迹几乎没有保存下来。余下的28座墓葬基本平面布列，相互间少有叠压。

墓地绝大多数墓葬结构一致，一般是先挖沙坑，坑中置棺具，然后在棺前后栽竖立木。南区一

至三层墓葬密集、上下反复叠压打破，很难判断墓室的范围，但多数墓葬特别是二、三层墓葬可依据棺前木柱上的遗痕推断出墓葬的开口位置，可知墓室的深度一般在1米左右。四、五层墓葬，位置低，沙质潮湿紧密，具有一定的直立性，所以部分墓葬墓室形状明确，基本呈2.5×1米余的长圆形，墓室普遍较深，最深的接近2米。墓葬均有棺具，一墓一棺。木棺由胡杨木制成的侧板、两挡、盖板拼合而成，均无底板。木棺上普遍覆盖着牛皮，最多的覆盖五六层，有的还盖有毛织物，牛皮上中部多放一把红柳枝及芦苇一支。

木棺前常竖立不同形制的立木，棺后竖红柳棍或细的胡杨木棍。棺前立木因死者性别不同而有区别，男性棺前立木似桨，桨面涂黑、桨柄涂红、柄端多刻有7道旋纹，"桨"的大小差别很大，最高的3米多，最宽的0.8米左右。女性棺前立木基本呈柱体，形制上也有不同，有的为上下均匀的多棱形木柱，有的上部为粗的多棱柱、下部则为细的圆柱，木柱端头均涂红、缠一段毛绳，绳下固定草束。两种立木的象征意义已很明晰：柱体象征男根，"桨"象征女阴。多数墓葬在墓室的最前端再立一

木柱上悬挂牛头
Ox Head Hanging on Wooden Pole

根高约3～5米的粗木柱，木柱露出地表的部分涂红，成为醒目的墓葬标志物。在这些粗木柱根部多置放一把由芦苇、骆驼刺、麻黄或甘草等干旱区植物组成的草束，草束中夹粗芦苇杆和羊腿骨，旁侧放草篓。

一棺一般葬敛一人，头向基本朝向东方，仰身直卧，头戴毡帽，身裹宽大的毛织斗篷，腰围毛织腰衣，足蹬短靴。除随身衣物、项饰、腕饰外，每墓必在斗篷外置一件极具工巧的显示几何花纹的草编篓。一些特别的随葬品，可能与墓主人的身份、地位有关，如随葬品丰富的男性墓中常见的嵌骨雕人面像的木杆形器、夹条石的蹄状木器、木雕的长蛇、彩绘木牌，还有男、女性墓中都随葬的凸显大鼻子的小型木雕人面像、额面切齐的大牛头等。

墓地发现少量结构特殊的泥壳木棺墓，和一般墓葬相比，泥壳木棺墓规模大，结构复杂，亦采用独木舟形木

男性墓的棺前立木
Wooden Item Erected in Front of A Male's Coffin

女性墓的棺前立木
Wooden Item Erected in Front of A Female's Coffin

棺，棺中葬一人，棺上再竖立木板，拼合成长方形的木板室，木板室中放置木雕人像，插有青石棒的裹皮角状器、木罐、草编篓、盘等，木板室口部盖草帘、搭绕草绳，然后抹泥，最后在这种泥外壳的木棺周围栽竖6或8根高约5米左右的木柱，木柱围成直径2米余的柱圈，柱上涂红，柱端悬挂牛头。发掘过程中，在这些木柱圈内及周围堆积中采集大量牛头、羊头。发掘的4座泥壳木棺墓，墓主均为成年女性，这似乎表示出女性在当时社会中具有特殊的地位。

墓地东北，发现了贝格曼当年据向导奥尔得克的口述而标注的"木房"。经过发掘，发现这是一座不同寻常的特殊墓葬，可惜已严重被破坏。这座墓葬由木构的长方形墓室和梯形的墓道组成，墓室面积7平方米左右，深（高）1.5米。由多棱形粗木柱和宽平的木板构筑，分前、后室。室内壁板以红、黑色涂绘几何纹样，室外壁蒙多层牛皮。围绕墓室堆垒有大量碎泥块，墓室前壁两侧整齐码放7层牛头。墓道结构简单，由侧放的木板、木柱围成，

揭取棺盖板后俯视木棺
Top View of Coffin after Removing its Cover

男性死者头前插木杆形器上镶嵌骨雕人面像
Bone Human Mask Inlaid on Wooden Item in Front of A Male's Head

泥壳木棺墓木板室中出土木雕人像
Wooden Human Sculpture from Timber Chamber
of Mud Burial with Wooden Coffin

泥壳木棺墓木板室中遗物
Remains from Timber Chamber of
Mud Burial with Wooden Coffin

泥壳木棺墓俯视
Top View of Mud Burial with Wooden Coffin

随葬品的大鼻子木雕人面像
Big-nosed Wooden Human Mask

木屋式墓葬全景
Full View of Hut-shaped Burial

木屋式墓葬盖板上彩绘
Color Painting on Wall of Hut-shaped Burial

前面耸立一根刻有旋纹的木柱。在墓室底部的位置发现1件圆形石质权杖头、2件骨雕人面像、1件铜质镜形器，在墓室上部及周围扰沙中频繁发现牛头和羊头，计有百余件。这应该是小河墓地发掘墓葬中规格最高的墓，它采用特殊的墓制埋藏在墓地墓葬区外独立的地方，并拥有独特的随葬品。因为盗扰严重，墓内不见尸骨，但据贝氏介绍，奥尔得克曾在这一"木房"中挖出一具女尸。

从发掘看，南区一至三层墓葬文化特征十分接近，而四、五两层墓葬文化特征相对一致，由此可将南区的墓葬分为上、下两组，这两组墓葬之间的区别较为明显。南区各层平面布局基本清晰，一般是由墓地中部向外围埋葬。第二层居中位置是一座男性墓，随葬品丰富、特殊；第三层几乎不见规格明显较高的墓葬；第四、五两层各以一座埋葬着女性的泥壳木棺墓为核心布列墓葬，由泥棺和周围木柱圈组成的遗构形式看，这是同层位墓葬中的一座具有重要祭祀功能的墓葬。北区墓葬由早到晚的整体情况不明，但从残存的少量墓葬看，它与南区四、五层墓葬文化面貌接近，但在墓葬布局上则存在区别，北区可能普遍存在有用木柱圈围起来的泥壳木棺组成的祭祀遗构，值得注意的是这里的泥壳木棺中所葬者，先是女性，后来可能出现了男性。

发掘前，对墓地表面散落的棺板进行统计，可知小河墓地上层的一百多座墓葬已完全被破坏，完整保留下来经过科学发掘的墓葬只是原来整个墓地的一半。由遗存反映的文化特征，参考文化面貌与此有密切关系的孔雀河古墓沟青铜时代墓地所测 ^{14}C 数据，初步推测小河墓地的年代大致在公元前2000 年左右，小河墓地发掘采集了出土于不同层位的大量的测年标本，随着小河墓地的进一步研究，参考测年数据，对墓地的年代会有一个科学的结论。

（供稿：伊弟利斯 李文瑛）

The Xiaohe cemetery is located approximately 4 km east of a small river, a southern branch of the Kongqi River southwest of Lop-Nur, Xinjiang. During the period from 2002 to 2005, the Institute of Archaeology of Xinjiang Uygur Autonomous Region fully excavated the Xiaohe cemetery, exposing 167 burials and yielding thousands of precious artifacts. The setting of the cemetery is an oval sand mound, which is over 7 m in height, 74 m in length, and about 35 m in width. The cemetery is divided by a wooden railing into two districts. In the south district, there are 139 burials piled up in five layers; in the north district, however, most of the burials were destroyed and only 28 burials have been preserved. Most of the burials are similar in structure: a sand pit was first dug for the coffin to be placed in, then vertical wooden items were erected at the two ends of the coffin. Each burial was furnished with one coffin. Made of *huyang*, a diversiform-leaved poplar, the coffins were shaped like a canoe without a bottom and covered with oxhide. An oar-shaped wooden item was erected in front of coffins belonging to a male and a multiphase pole in front of those belonging to a female, symbolizing the female sex organ and the male sex organ, respectively. At the most front of the coffin, also erected was a high and thick wooden pole fully painted red. Usually a coffin had only one occupant, who was arranged extended and facing up, with a felt hat and a felt cloak on, and a grass basket attached to the outside of the cloak.

The Xiaohe cemetery is preliminarily dated to around 2000 BC.

安阳殷墟
殷代大墓及车马坑

LARGE TOMBS AND CHARIOT PITS
AT YINXU IN ANYANG, HENAN

2004年11月，安阳市文物钻探队在安钢第二炼钢厂西南部基建占地范围内进行文物勘探，其中3座较大型墓葬和7座车马坑引人注目。此地位于殷墟保护范围西部边缘处。中国社会科学院考古研究所安阳工作站及时向国家文物局填报了发掘执照申请表并与安阳市文物工作队联合组成发掘队对该处遗迹进行抢救性发掘。发掘工作自2005年元月开始，于6月22日全部结束。

墓葬位于发掘地点东偏北部，3座大墓由西向东编号依次为：2005AGM11、2005AGM12、2005AGM13。形制分别为"中"字形、"甲"字形、"中"字形。车马坑共7座，编号2005AGM1～M7。M7紧靠M11墓道西南处，其余6座位于墓葬西南部约40米处。M1～M5呈北偏东12°，南北一线排列，坑距0.5～0.6米。M6位于M5东偏北处，相距约5米。从平面布局及发掘出土遗物判断，这7座车马坑应与偏北处3座大墓有陪葬关系。

3座墓葬的形制、面积、埋葬葬具、深度及所代表的墓主人身份等级，无法与西北冈王陵级大墓相比，在殷墟只能称之为较大型墓葬。但墓主人身份也应为当时上层贵族。

M11平面呈"中"字形，墓室上口长7.5、宽5米，南墓道长30、宽2～2.4米，斜坡式，坡度40°。墓室北置台阶式短墓道。墓底距地表11.5米。该墓被盗严重，仅存少量遗物：可复原陶罐、蚌饰、海贝、铜镞、残骨锥及仅存的椁底板。但在墓室北部二层台上发现3条骨片，其中1条有绿松石镶嵌的文字16个，下部残，这种以绿松石镶嵌成文字的表现形式在殷墟极为罕见。

M12平面呈"甲"字形，墓室上口长5、宽3.8米，墓道长12.5、宽2.3～2.5米，呈台阶式踏步。墓深9.5米。遗物仅见经盗扰过的铜镞、海贝、蚌饰、残铜戈。在墓道与墓室相接处，殉有1人2狗，铜铃置于狗骨架上。

M13位于最东处，是3座墓中最大的一座。墓平面呈"中"字形，墓室上口长9.5、宽8米，南墓道残长9、宽2.8～3.1米，斜坡式45°；北墓道长8.3、宽1.9～2.5米。墓东西各设一小墓道，呈台阶式，长2.5、宽1米，呈假"亚"字形。该墓早期被盗，在填土中发现以红、黑漆为主色调的雕花棺(椁)板，在墓壁西南部二层台上发现铜戈10余件、石磬1件、铜镞20余枚、陶弹丸100余枚。墓

M11 墓室全景（由南向北）
Full View of Tomb M11 Chamber (from south to north)

M13 墓道内殉狗及墓底椁板痕迹（由南向北）
Sacrificial Dog in Tomb Passage and Remaining Signs of *guo*–Coffin in Tomb M13 (from south to north)

M11 出土的带字骨片
Bone Tablet with Characters from Tomb M11

车马坑 M3 出土青铜短剑
Bronze Short Sword from Chariot Pit M3

底椁板保存完好。

车马坑 7 座。

M1～M5，5 辆马车马头向东有序排列，每车葬马 2 匹，马侧身置于车辕两旁。每辆车都有殉人，M1、M2 各殉 1 人，殉人置于车厢后。M3 殉 1 人，置于车的右侧。M4、M5 分别殉葬 2 人，分置于车厢右侧与厢后。5 辆车、马均有不同的装饰和络饰。自南向北 M1、M2 车、马的装饰较简单，与殷墟常见的车马装饰无异，车轴处有铜辖和铜軎，车厢下及踵门处均有铜饰件，车辕两侧有铜角形器，马头处有铜轭、铜镳，络饰为大、小型铜泡。M4、M5 马头络饰较为豪华，M4 虽为各式铜泡，但繁缛中显规整。M5 马具及络饰用加工成长方形或椭圆形蚌片串联而成，美观而精巧，在殷墟众多车马装饰中也难得一见。

M3 居中，在车厢前部右侧发现 1 件青铜短剑及 1 件带孔磨石。青铜短剑部分压在车厢下，长度 30～35 厘米，短剑柄端圈底镂空，柄中饰数道刻划弦纹，整器具北方草原风格。车厢前左侧发现一簇

M13出土的雕花漆棺（椁）板
Carved Lacquer Coffin
Planks from Tomb M13

铜镞，约30枚，隐约可见箭杆、箭囊痕迹。5辆车马虽异穴埋葬，但排列规整、间隔有序，应是同一时期埋入的。车马配饰、随葬物的差异可能反映了车的不同用途。

车马坑发掘清理完毕，已整体装箱搬运至异地保护。

关于大墓和车马坑的关系：M13在墓道中殉葬的马头上发现了与M5马头装饰完全相同的蚌片，以及相同的层位，推测东北部3座大墓与这批车马坑年代相同或接近。

（供稿：刘忠伏 孔德铭）

车马坑M1~M5发掘清理现场
Excavation at the Site of Five Chariot Pits M1–M5

车马坑M1~M5全景
Panoramic View of Five Chariot Pits M1–M5

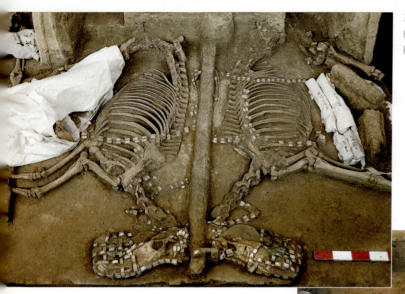

车马坑 M5 马头络饰及马身佩饰
Horse Head Ornaments and Body
Pendants in Chariot Pit M5

车马坑 M5 (由东向西)
Chariot Pit M5 (from east to west)

From November 2004 to June 2005, a field survey was carried out at Yinxu (Ruin of Yin) jointly by the Anyang Work Station of the Institute of Archaeology, the Chinese Academy of Social Sciences and the Archaeological Team of Anyang City, which was followed by the excavation of the identified three large tombs and seven chariot pits.

The three tombs are located in the northeastern part of the excavation area. Judging from the structure and scale of the tombs, the status of the occupants should be that of high ranking aristocrats of the Shang society, although these tombs were obviously not comparable to the royal graves at Xibeigang. All the tombs had been hunted, but some important artifacts were left, including restorable pots, bronze *ge*-daggers, shell ornaments, sea shells, bronze arrow-heads, *qing*-chimestones, and delicate lacquered coffin planks. One precious item is the bone tablet which is inscribed with 16 characters and inlaid with turquoise stones. The inscriptions record a Shang King's activities on the day of *ren*-wu when he went to hunting, captured rhinoceroses, and granted rewards.

According to the burial patterns of large tombs and chariot pits at Yinxu, the identified seven chariot pits should be attendant burials of the large tombs. Of them, five chariots were arranged in a straight line in the north - south direction, and the heads of the horses in the pits were all directed to the east. Every chariot was also accompanied by a sacrificial human attendant. The shape of the chariots and the type of the horses are the common ones at Yinxu, but the chariot decoration and horse ornaments are distinctive. The ornaments on the horses in Pit M5 were attached with delicately processed shell slices instead of the bronze semi-spherical buttons commonly seen in other chariot pits, presenting a luxurious style. In Pit M3, a bronze short sword and over 30 bronze arrow-heads were placed in front of the chariot in the center, reflecting a distinctive function of this central chariot.

All of the chariot pits have been excavated and removed as a whole from the site for the purpose of conservation.

陕西岐山周公庙遗址

ZHOUGONGMIAO SITE IN QISHAN, SHAANXI

周公庙遗址位于陕西省岐山县城以北约7.5公里的凤凰山南麓，东距著名的周原遗址27公里。2003年12月，北京大学考古文博学院在此调查时，发现了两片计有55字的周人刻辞卜甲，引起了学术界的极大关注。为了解该遗址不同时期、特别是商周时期文化遗存的具体年代、分布范围及其文化性质，由陕西省考古研究所和北京大学考古文博学院于2004年2月联合组成的周公庙考古队，对该遗址进行了大范围的调查、大面积的钻探与抢救性的发掘。两年来对该遗址的布局和年代等问题都有了初步的了解。

经钻探发现商周时期墓葬900余座，分布于相对集中的5处墓地。

陵坡墓地发现的大型墓葬最为引人瞩目。共发现墓葬37座，其中具4条墓道的10座，带3条、2条、1条墓道的各4座，另有无墓道陪葬墓15座。尤其是4条墓道和3条墓道的发现，填补了以往西周墓葬形制的空白。该墓地应是目前所知西周时期最高等级的墓葬群。在陵坡墓地的东、西、北三面，还发现了长达1500米的环绕于墓地外围的夯土墙，

墙宽5米，个别地方墙体残存高度2.5米。墙体和陵坡墓地的关系还有待进一步的确定。

白草坡墓地是一处以中型墓葬为主的贵族墓地，共发现墓葬200余座。除3座带1条墓道者外，其余墓葬均为长方形竖穴土圹墓，其中墓口长在3米以上者约占三分之二。

樊村等其他墓地均以小型墓葬为主，中型墓葬少见。

在陵坡墓地发掘了2座带墓道的大墓。已发掘的M18，墓室长6.8、宽6.4米，东墓道长12.4、宽0.9米，西墓道长7.5、宽1.3米，南墓道长17.6、宽4.2米；北墓道长17.7、宽0.9米。虽多经盗扰，仍出土大量的青铜器、玉石器、原始瓷器等。陵坡墓地M32中出土大量原始瓷器，初步辨识出器类12种，个体数达20多件，是目前所知西周墓葬中出土原始瓷器较多的一座。其中1件圈足底部有刻字，是现知最早的标款瓷器。在白草坡墓地发掘中型墓葬3座，出土2件带铭铜器及多件玉器。在樊村墓地共清理墓葬29座、马坑2座。出土随葬品有陶器、玉器及近百件小件铜器。墓葬年代多不晚于

西周早期。推测墓主应是低等级贵族和一般平民。通过这些墓葬的发掘，初步了解了周公庙遗址各等级墓地的年代与性质。

共清理3座西周时期的卜甲坑，分别位于白草坡墓地南边与大型夯土建筑群的南端。出土卜甲700余片，其中有刻辞者90余片，字数最多的一块卜甲刻辞37字，是所有西周卜甲中字数最多者。初步辨识出刻辞495字，约占现知全部西周甲骨刻辞字数的三分之一。刻辞内容多与军事、纪事有关，出现最多的人名为"周公"，地名中以"周"与"新邑"最为常见，"唐"、"薄姑"等地名虽仅各1见，但均系首见于西周甲骨文中。月相刻辞"哉死霸"亦为第一次发现。通过对甲骨坑堆积状况、出土陶片年代特征、卜甲刻辞内容等方面的分析，

夯土墙西墙
Western Section of
Stamped-earth Wall

陵坡墓地M18鸟瞰
Top View of Tomb M18
in Lingpo Cemetery

樊村墓地发掘现场
Excavation on Site
of Fancun Cemetery

庙王村西甲骨坑
Oracle-bone Pit West
of Miaowangcun Village

卜骨
Oracle Bone

卜骨刻辞
Oracle Bone Inscriptions

卜骨刻辞
Oracle Bone Inscription

夯土建筑基址局部
Partial View of
Stamped-earth Archi-
tectural Foundation

初步判定周公庙遗址卜甲的年代可能为西周早期。这是继1976年岐山县凤雏甲骨之后的又一重大发现，为研究当时的卜甲整治、刻辞文例及西周早期历史的相关问题提供了直接文字资料。

共发现并局部清理了2处作坊遗址。其中铸铜作坊位于陵坡墓地以南的马尾沟东岸，制陶作坊位于2003年卜甲发现地点。

对铸铜作坊进行了小规模的发掘，清理面积为128平方米，共清理出与制铜有关的陶窑1座、房址1座及灰坑10余座，出土了大量陶范。陶范种类有鼎、簋等容器范，刀、镞等兵器范，马衔、泡、銮铃等车马器范。工具有陶管、砺石等。从陶范形制及共存陶器年代特征分析，该处作坊的年代为西周初期，其上限有早至先周晚期的可能性。

刻字原始瓷器
Proto-porcelain Ware with Inscribed Character

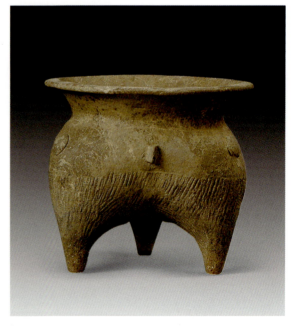

陶鬲
Pottery *li*

松石蝉
Turquoise Cicadas

玉璜
Jade *huang*–segment

玉柄形器
Jade Handle–shaped Object

玉鸟
Jade Bird

簋范
Pottery Mould for Making
Bronze *gui*–container

建筑用瓦
Architectural tile

骨笄
Bone Hairpin

石磬
Chimestone

玉器出土情况
Exposure of Jade Object

刀范
Pottery Mould for Making Bronze Knife

铜簋
Bronze gui-container

制陶作坊处的发掘面积近150平方米，发现了集中分布的4座陶窑。所见陶窑均为半倒烟式，窑床以上部分均已残。从窑内陶器形制及相关层位关系判断，这些陶窑的使用年代应为商周之际或稍早。在此处还清理灰坑46座，复杂的层位关系及丰富的出土物，使商代晚期与西周早期关中西部地区的考古学文化编年体系得以进一步完善，弥补了一些以往认识上的空白。特别是卜甲坑H45中记时刻辞、称"王"刻辞与商周之际的陶器共存，或可作为讨论商周分界的重要依据。

在制陶作坊遗址以北，还调查发现了制石工具，这为进一步寻找周公庙遗址的制石作坊提供了线索。

大型夯土建筑群的发现是周公庙遗址考古的另一重要收获，这些大型建筑基址主要集中分布于陵坡墓地以南，在白草坡墓地以南区域亦有零星发现。

在建筑基址的周围，采集到大量的砖和瓦，特别是空心砖的发现，证明这些建筑基址的较高规格。

2005年秋冬季，在夯土建筑群的北部发掘了1500平方米。所见大型夯土建筑基址的建造年代不早于先周晚期，废弃年代不晚于西周早期偏晚阶段。建筑基址地面以上部分及基槽上部多被破坏，除发现一段排水沟和少量柱洞外，其余所见多为建筑基槽的下部。基槽由40余块夯土块组成，这些夯土块均为长方形，大小不一，形制有别，多数面积在15～35平方米之间。通过此次的发掘，对西周时期大型夯土建筑的营建技术和过程取得了更进一步的了解，同时也为最终解决遗址的性质问题积累了必要的资料。

两年来的考古工作，大体建立了周公庙遗址较为详细的考古学文化编年体系与文化谱系，初步了解了遗址中心区域的聚落结构，为周公庙遗址相关学术问题研究提供了重要资料，并为该遗址的有效保护与长远工作规划提供了科学的依据。虽然暂时还没有找到直接的证据回答周公庙遗址的性质问题，但现有的发现已有足够的理由使我们相信，该遗址将来的考古工作必将对西周考古与历史的研究产生积极的推动作用。

（供稿：徐天进）

The Zhougongmiao (Temple of Duke Zhou) site is located at the southern foot of the Fenghuangshan (Phoenix Mountains) approximately 7.5 km north of the town of Qishan County, Shaanxi Province. Since February 2004, the Zhougongmiao Archaeological Team, which is jointly organized by the School of Archaeology and Museology of Beijing (Peking) University and the Shaanxi Provincial Institute of Archaeology, has identified 901 graves of the Shang-Zhou period in five cemeteries at the Zhougongmiao site. Of the five cemeteries, the Lingpo cemetery is the highest ranking burial complex of the Zhou period so far found to our knowledge. Within the Lingpo cemetery, ten graves have been found with four tomb passages, four with three passages, four with two passages, and four with one passage. Around the Lingpo cemetery, a stamped-earth wall 1,500 m long has been discovered.

Three oracle-bone pits were excavated at the site. These pits yielded more than 700 oracle turtle shells, including over 90 shells with inscriptions, and 495 characters have now been deciphered. Two workshop sites were identified and partially excavated. The bronze workshop is dated to the transitional period from the Shang to the Zhou, and a large amount of pottery moulds and bronze-making implements have been unearthed from this workshop site. At the pottery workshop site, four closely distributed pottery kilns were identified. The production time of the kilns should be dated to the transitional period from the Shang to the Zhou or earlier. Furthermore, a large stamped-earth architectural complex has been identified through surface survey and auger drilling, and a size of 1,500 sq m excavated at the northern end of the complex. What has been exposed from the excavation is the lower portion of a foundation trench, which was composed of over 40 cross-banded stamped-earth chunks. The construction date of the foundation is no earlier than the late pre-Zhou period, and the abandonment date of the structure is no later than the late phase of the early Western Zhou period.

铜节约
Bronze Harness Fitting

铜銮铃
Bronze Chariot Bell

铜锛
Bronze *ben*–adze

铜衡末饰
Bronze Yoke–end Fitting

山西绛县
横水西周墓地

WESTERN ZHOU CEMETERY
AT HENGSHUI, JIANGXIAN COUNTY, SHANXI

2004 年 4 月，山西绛县横水镇横北村北坡一带出现严重的盗掘古墓活动。7 月，运城市文物局组织钻探，11 月对被盗墓葬进行发掘。12 月中旬，由山西省考古研究所等单位组成横水考古队，经国家文物局批准开始正式发掘。目前已经清理墓葬 110 多座。

在已发掘的墓葬中，M1、M2 保存完好，根据这两座墓葬形制、随葬器物、铜器铭文可知，墓主人为文献未载的西周中期的倗伯夫妇。此外，在 M1 中发现了十分珍贵的荒帷遗迹，并对其实施了保护搬迁。

两座墓口距现地表 1.8 米。均为带斜坡墓道的竖穴土圹木椁墓，墓室在东，墓道在西。从平面上看，墓室与墓道基本呈"一"字形。

M1 方向 272°，长 26.65、深 15.28 米。椁室长 4.3、宽 3、深 3.15 米。二层台上放置一辆车。葬具为一椁二棺。椁室是木结构，整体平面为"Ⅱ"字形。墓主人头向西，仰身直肢，双手交叠置于小腹上。外棺东端的棺椁之间有 3 具殉人骨架，以苇席裹包。随葬品主要有车马器、陶器、漆木器、青铜礼器和玉器。

M2 方向与 M1 一致，东西长 23.8、西宽 3.74、东宽 2.84、深 14.4 米。墓室口长 5.5、宽 2.84~

3.04 米。一椁两棺，椁室呈"Ⅱ"字形，长 4.1、宽 3.14、高 2.27 米。椁盖上西部有一车，墓主人头向西，俯身直肢葬。棺椁间有殉人 4 个。随葬品主要有车马器、青铜礼器和玉器。

本次最重要的发现是 M1 中的荒帷。先秦史籍《周礼》、《仪礼》、《礼记》等对荒帷有多处记载，周代的高级贵族墓里多使用荒帷。荒帷如棺罩，覆盖在棺上，是真正意义上的饰棺之物。荒帷又称墙柳，《仪礼·既夕礼》郑玄注云："饰柩为设墙柳也……墙有布帷，柳有布荒。"贾公彦疏曰："设墙柳也者，即加帷荒也。"《周礼·天官·缝人》郑玄注："孝子既见启棺，犹见亲之身，既载饰而以形，遂以葬，若存时居于帷幄而加文秀。"可知荒帷的设置乃是对死者生前居室中帷幄一类设施的模仿，但另一方面，在出殡时荒帷还可起到"华道路"的作用，如《丧大礼》郑玄注云："饰棺者，以华道路及圹中，不欲众恶其亲也"。

从荒帷出土的情况看，当时是套盖在外棺上，但在下葬之后，椁室多次进水淤土，位于棺椁之间的荒帷便被淤土封住了，这为荒帷的保存提供了必要的条件。

西、北面的荒帷保存相对较好，现存高约 160 厘米，南面的荒帷上部已塌落，现存高约 120~130

墓葬分布情况
Distribution of Tombs

M1 俯视
Overview of Tomb M1

M1椁室（由东向西）
Outer Coffin of Tomb M1
(from east to west)

M1 出土青铜器
Bronze Vessels from
Tomb M1

厘米，东面的荒帷保存最差，基本仅剩下部底裙的局部，高约10多厘米，保存的总面积有10平方米左右。荒帷整体是红色的丝织品，由两幅横拼而成，上下有扉边，每幅宽80厘米左右，总高约180～220厘米，布幅拼接的地方有明显的接缝。在织物上有精美的的刺绣图案，图案主题是凤鸟。北壁的图案保存较完整，至少观察到3组大小不同的鸟纹图案，每组图案中间是一个大凤鸟的侧面，昂首、大勾喙、圆眼、冠高耸、翅上扬、尾下卷、硕健粗壮的腿、利爪、翅和冠以特别夸张的手法作大回

旋，线条流畅。在大凤鸟的前后，上下排列多只小凤鸟，造型与大凤鸟基本相像，只是更加含蓄。在织物接缝的地方有图案错位和颠倒现象，可见当时是先在布上刺绣出图案，然后才拼接成整幅。此外，同荒帷相伴的其他饰棺、束棺和下棺等遗物痕迹也在发掘中清理了出来。

根据钻探，基本确定了墓地范围南北长约200、东西宽约150米，面积约30000平方米，共发现墓葬300余座。根据墓葬分布情况，对存在被盗危险的重要墓葬进行全面揭露，发掘面积8500

M1 出土铜盉
He-container from Tomb M1

M1 出土铜鼎
Ding-tripod from Tomb M1

M1 玉器出土情况
Unearthing Jades from Tomb M1

M1 北壁荒帷鸟纹
Bird Design on *huang wei*
over North Wall of Coffin

M1 西壁荒帷
Huang wei over West
Wall of Coffin

平方米，共发现墓葬188座，车马坑21座。其中有97座为小型墓葬，其余为大中型墓葬，发现1座带墓道的大型墓葬，墓室和墓道呈"一"字形。大型墓葬或为对子墓，或为单个墓，皆陪葬有车马坑；中型墓葬亦或为对子墓，或为单个墓，多数陪葬有车马坑或马坑。小型墓葬多数集中分布在墓地的西部，少数分布于墓地东部或南部，多为单个墓葬。

此外，在该墓地发掘过程中，发现在多数大中型墓葬的墓口外东侧方向或四角，有长方形、圆形或椭圆形的小坑遗迹，经解剖证明是柱洞，分属14座墓葬。另有5座墓葬的墓口外四角发现有四个小坑遗迹。该遗迹现象在西周墓葬考古发掘中为第一次发现，其中有一部分是柱洞，一部分是通到墓葬内的斜洞，至于这些柱洞和斜洞的功能还有待进一步分析确定。

截至目前，发掘出土的随葬器物有铜、陶、蚌、贝、漆、玉器等，共206件组。

M2随葬铜器16件，有鼎3，簋、尊、觯、盉、爵、卣、瓿、盘各1，以及甬钟5件；M1随葬铜器25件，有鼎5、簋5、盉2、壶2、盘2、觯1、瓿1、盉1、甬钟5件。根据铜器形制以及M1出土荒帷的鸟纹图案看，M1、M2的时代当为西周中期，约穆王后期。

两座墓出土的青铜礼器中各有8件带有铭文，其中M2的2件铜鼎和1件瓿上有"倗伯"为自己做器的铭文，M1则在4件铜器上有"倗伯乍毕姬宝旅鼎（盘、簋、瓿）"铭，表明M2的墓主是倗伯，M1的墓主是倗伯夫人。

（供稿：宋建忠 吉琨璋 田建文 谢尧亭）

M1 发掘结束后椁室状态
Condition of the Outer Coffin after Excavation

M2出土青铜器
Unearthed Bronzes

M2俯视
Top View of Tomb M2

M2出土铜爵
Bronze *jue*-cup from Tomb M2

M2 出土铜卣
Bronze *you*–container
from Tomb M2

铜卣盖内铭文
Inscriptions inside Lid of
Bronze *you*–Container

In December 2004, the Hengshui Archaeological Team organized by the Shanxi Provincial Institute of Archaeology conducted a rescue excavation of ancient tombs at Hengbei village in Hengshui, Jiangxian County, Shanxi, exposing over 110 tombs. Of them, Tombs M1 and M2 were vertical earth pits connected to a straight sloping passage and furnished with wooden inner and outer coffins. Inferred from the tomb structure, buried artifacts, and especially the bronze inscriptions of the two tombs, the occupants of Tomb M1 and M2 were Count Peng and his wife, a never before documented couple from the middle Western Zhou period. It can be inferred from their status that the grave site at Hengshui was a cemetery of the Peng State in the Western Zhou.

The most important discovery during this excavation was the remains of *huang wei*, a textile cover laid over the inner coffin. In pre-Qin documents, *huang wei* was repeatedly mentioned and commonly used by high ranking aristocrats of the Western Zhou, but it has never been identified before in numerous Western Zhou and Eastern Zhou tombs by archaeologists. This discovery therefore has finally revealed the true face of Western Zhou *huang wei*.

陕西韩城
梁带村两周遗址

ZHOU SITE AT LIANGDAICUN
IN HANCHENG, SHAANXI

韩城市位于陕西省东部，地处关中平原与陕北黄土高原过渡地带。梁带村隶属韩城市昝村镇，位于市区东北7公里黄河西岸的台地上，遗址紧临黄河。

2004年12月～2005年3月，渭南市文物保护考古研究所、韩城市文物旅游局在梁带村村北进行了小范围的勘探，发现三处古墓葬。受陕西省文物局的委派，陕西省考古研究所于2005年4月起对梁带村及其周围的古遗址进行了调查和勘探，共发现两周时期的墓葬103座，车马坑17座。在103座墓葬中，有30余座墓中发现有朱砂和塌陷现象，由此看出，这应是一处保存较好的贵族墓地。同时还对墓地的四界进行了抽样勘探，确定梁带村村北一带为一处大型墓地，面积约为330000平方米。经国家文物局批准，陕西省考古研究所抢救性地发掘了车马坑1座（K1）、墓葬3座（M19、M26和M27）。

K1车马坑为口大底小的南北向长方形土圹。坑口长5.1、宽4.2、深4.8米。坑内发现马车构件、青铜车饰和殉牲的马、狗骨架等，其中清理出车轮7个，车舆3乘，辕木3根，另有衡木、轴木、车轭等。5匹马骨架摆放整齐，未发现马匹有挣扎的痕迹，当是被处死后放置坑内。从车、马摆放位置看，其填埋过程为：先在坑底有序地放置马匹，后在马匹上放置拆解后的马车构件。出土的青铜车饰中有2套辖、𫐄以及2件轭首、4件轭足等。其中轭首形制少见，上部有向上伸出的舌形弯铃底座，两面饰蝉纹；下部呈倒梯形，略束腰，上下贯通，两面饰高浮雕兽面纹，高10、宽11.8厘米。

M19平面呈"甲"字形，墓道斜坡状，长26、宽4米。墓室长6.6、宽5.6、深11.8米。东距M27约20米，方向为215°。

墓葬的棺椁结构为一椁两棺。椁室南北长4.7、东西宽3.2米，以木板和方木搭建。外棺髹漆，长3.03、宽1.65米。东、北侧板彩绘保存较好，内壁为波浪状红彩；外壁为红彩折线、锯齿纹组合图案。内棺长2.45、宽0.9米。墓主骨架粉化，周身施撒朱砂。

椁室内装饰品丰富，椁周壁及东西两侧板间悬挂大量串饰。组合较清楚的共305组，计出土铜鱼609、玛瑙珠管1800、海贝520、陶珠3900、石坠800余枚。4件片状青铜翣，在外棺顶板上与串饰叠压平置，翣上部为"山"字形，下部为矩形，高58、宽68、厚不及0.1厘米，已完整提取。在外棺侧板的外壁发现10件龙纹镂空铜环，东西两侧各有对称的4件，南北两端各有对称的1件，铜环直

K1出土青铜车轭首
Two Bronze Yoke-saddle Finials from Chariot Pit K1

车马坑（K1）全景
Comprehensive View of Chariot Pit K1

M19 外棺顶板上的铜翣及串饰
Bronze Coffin Ornaments and Strung Ornaments
on Top Board of Outer Coffin in Tomb M19

M19 出土铜鬲的铭文
Inscriptions on Bronze *li*–tripod
from Tomb M19

M19 出土青铜簋
Bronze *gui*–container

M19 出土玉鸟、玉贝及玻璃珠组成的串饰
String of Ornaments Composed of Jade Birds,
Jade Shells and Glass Beads from Tomb M19

M19 出土青铜鼎
Bronze *ding*–tripod

M19发现的彩绘漆箱痕迹
Lacquer Chest Painted
with Color from Tomb M19

M26青铜器出土情形
Exposure of Bronze Objects
in Tomb M26

M26出土玉猪龙
Jade Pig-dragon from Tomb M26

径19.5厘米。

在椁室西部和南部发现青铜礼器,计鼎4、簋4、鬲4、壶2、盉1、甗1、盘1、盂1,其中3件鼎形制、纹样相同,大小相次,另一件鼎略有差异,立耳,垂腹,蹄形足,腹饰高浮雕垂鳞纹,制作精美,口径27.8、通高25.8厘米。铜鬲口沿面上铸有铭文,内容有二:一是"内(芮)太子作铸鬲子子孙孙永宝用享";二是"内(芮)公作铸鬲子子孙孙永宝用享"。

墓主随葬玉器66件,其中的63件与玛瑙珠(管)442颗相间组成项饰、臂饰、腕饰和脚腕饰。在其腕部和臂部有四组串饰,由玉鸟、玉蚕、玉觿、玉贝、玉泡与玛瑙珠组成。另外还发现有瑗、玦、握、

M26 玉器出土情况
Exposure of Jade Pig-dragon in Tomb M26

琮、玉柄形器、牛首、鱼形饰等。

此外，在椁室内围绕外棺一周还发现漆器 18
件，有箱、盒、豆等。在椁室东部有彩绘漆箱顶板，
红底黑彩，图案清晰，色彩鲜艳。

M26 平面呈"甲"字形，墓道斜坡状，长 26、
宽 3.8 米。墓室长 7.1、宽 5.65、深 12.2 米。亦为
一椁两棺，该墓随葬品的最大特点为：青铜礼器制
作精，个体大；玉器种类全、数量多。青铜礼器共
计 23 件，以能反映墓葬等级的五鼎四簋最为重要；
玉器 500 余件，以组佩七璜联珠和梯形牌饰最引人
注目，另有玉猪龙、牙璧、玉人、虎、熊（残）、蝉、
蚕、龟、贝、鸟、握、匕等。M26 随葬玉器年代跨
度大、来源亦相当多元。据初步观察，有红山文化
的玉猪龙、龙山文化的素面玉璧、商代的龙纹玉
璜、西周的龙纹交尾玉璜，直至春秋的龙纹玉牌。
其中刻字牙璧的年代应不晚于商代。另外，高 14 厘
米的玉猪龙，从玉质和造型看，其属性为红山文
化，当为墓主的生前收藏。这可能是目前发现的红

山文化玉猪龙的最南分布，大大拓展了我们对红山
玉器的认识。

M27 平面为"中"字形，有南北两条墓道，
南墓道长 33.8 米；北墓道 17.3 米。墓室长 9、宽
7.3、深 13.2 米，墓向为 218°。

墓室的棺椁结构为一椁两棺。椁室南北长 5.7、
东西宽 4.4 米。椁顶板除中央正常塌陷外，保存完
好，22 块椁板横向铺设。顶板下发现有围绕外棺的
若干条朽断木痕，南北 4 四根、东西 7 根，这当为
棺罩痕迹。

在棺椁之间的东、西、南三面发现大量青铜车
马器；东、北椁壁有兵戈、钺等青铜；椁室东北部
发现 1 件漆木鼓（建鼓），鼓下已暴露 5 件编钟，鼓
南侧还发现 5 件形制巨大的编磬，这可能是目前已
知周代发现的最大编磬。青铜礼器多放置于东侧，
计有鼎、簋、甗、盘、壶、尊、卣、觯、爵等 20 件，
其中包括六鼎六簋。内棺墓主胸部至腹部放置 48
件金器，有剑鞘、三角龙纹带饰、兽首形带扣、龙、

M27椁室顶板
Top Board of *guo*-out coffin

M27 发现的漆器建鼓痕迹
Lacquer Drum on Stand from Tomb M27

镶、环、泡等，金器制作细腻、造型优美，保存完好。墓主随身佩戴和随葬的玉器有组佩七璜联珠以及琮、璧、圭、戈、镶、觿、梯形牌、鸟等近200件。

梁带村墓地的发掘工作仍在进行之中。梁带村墓地是关中东部首次发现的两周之际的诸侯国墓地，所发掘的三座大墓未被盗掘，出土了丰富的遗物，其意义不言而喻。

根据对三座墓葬的形制及出土青铜器、玉器分析，初步判断其年代为西周晚期——东周早期，最可能的年代为春秋早期。

关于墓葬的等级，根据以往发掘的晋侯墓地和虢国墓地的墓葬形制、规模和随葬品，特别是M27出土的大量金器、玉器和青铜礼器分析，梁带村三座带墓道的大墓当为诸侯级墓葬。

M19出土的青铜鬲口沿铸有"内（芮）太子"、"内（芮）公"的铭文，M19为代表的遗存属于芮国遗存的可能性较大。但根据《史记》三家注，春秋早期梁国地望在今韩城市境内，而芮国地望在今韩城以南约100公里的大荔县及附近。上述文化遗存从时空看，还不能完全排除属于梁国贵族墓地的可能性。所以梁带村墓地的具体国别尚有待下一步工作的确认，从某种程度上讲，即有赖于M27铜器铭文的发现。

（供稿：孙秉君 陈建凌 程蕊萍）

M27 发掘情况
Excavation at Tomb M27

M27 出土金剑鞘
Gold Scabbard from Tomb 27

M27 出土镶金玉鲽、人面虎身玉饰
Gold-inlaid Jade Archer's Thumb Ring and Jade Pendant with Human Face and Tiger Body from Tomb 27

Since April 2005, the Shaanxi Provincial Institute of Archaeology has been undertaking an archaeological survey and a subsequent excavation at Liangdaicun village in Hancheng City, Shaanxi Province. The survey along the bank of the Yellow River revealed a residential site and a cemetery dated to the Zhou period. The residential site is located north and east of the village, with a size of approximately 600,000 sq m; the cemetery is located north of the village, with a size of approximately 330,000 sq m. 103 graves and 17 chariot pits of the Zhou period were identified through auger drilling, including four large tombs with passages. It has been tentatively concluded that this burial complex is a well preserved high ranking aristocratic cemetery of the Zhou period.

Permitted by the State Administration of Cultural Heritage, excavations were carried out at three large tombs M19, M26, and M27 as well as at chariot pit K1. The three large tombs have not been hunted, the features and artifacts therefore are in good condition. A large amount of jade ornaments, bronze ritual and musical objects, and lacquered wooden objects were unearthed from the three large tombs. Tomb M27 is especially remarkable as 48 gold objects were unearthed from this burial. Judging from the structural scale as well as the quality and quantity of funerary objects of the three tombs, they are tentatively ranked to the level of feudal princes.

Based on the structural pattern of the tombs and the morphologies and decoration designs of the bronze chariot fittings, bronze ritual vessels, and jade ornaments, these remains are tentatively dated to the period between the late Western Zhou and the early Eastern Zhou, but most likely to the early Spring and Autumn period.

The bronze *li*-tripod unearthed from Tomb M19 bears inscriptions referring to Prince Rui and Duke Rui. This information provides an important clue that allows us to infer the feudal state identity of the Liangdaicun cemetery.

江苏句容、金坛
土墩墓考古发掘收获

ACHIEVEMENTS FROM EXCAVATIONS OF EARTH-MOUND-TOMBS IN JURONG AND JINTAN, JIANGSU

土墩墓是西周时期江南地区的一种特殊的埋葬方式，主要分布在苏南、皖南和浙江上海等长江下游一带。这种墓有坟丘而无墓穴，利用丘陵地带的山冈或平原上的高地，在地面上安置死者和随葬器物，然后堆积起未经夯打的馒头状土墩。每个墩内埋一墓或埋几座甚至十几座墓……

从20世纪70年代江苏句容开始正式发掘并命名、80年代浙江、安徽也发现土墩墓以来，由于各地发现的土墩结构异常复杂，是一墩一墓，还是一墩多墓？是平地掩埋还是竖穴挖坑？祭祀器物群与墓葬什么关系？诸多问题使土墩墓成为长期以来困扰南方考古学界的谜。

2005年江苏宁常、镇溧高速公路穿越句容、金坛土墩墓特别密集的区域，2005年4~9月，江苏省文物局组织南京博物院、南京市博物馆、镇江市博物馆、常州市博物馆、南京大学、南京师范大学以及溧水、溧阳、句容和金坛文管会、博物馆等单位共同参加，由80余名专业人员分别组成8支考古队同时对高速公路沿线的土墩墓进行规模空前的抢救性考古发掘。发掘工作由南京博物院主持，先后调查发现土墩墓46座，其中被高速公路建设彻底破坏6座，实际发掘土墩40座。共清理墓葬233座、祭祀器物群（坑）229个、丧葬建筑14座，出土文物3800多件。

确认一墩一墓与一墩多墓并存

在本次发掘中可以确定的一墩一墓有3座墩子，一墩多墓有28座。一墩一墓的土墩一般除中部的一座墓葬外，在其四周不同层面上放置数量不等的祭祀器物群（坑），如天王东边山D2、薛埠上水D2、薛埠磨盘林场D1等。一墩多墓的土墩一般除中部的一座墓葬外，在其四周不同层面上再埋有至少1座墓葬，而句容浮山果园D29，除中心墓葬外，在周边还先后埋有44座墓葬，这是目前发现的在一座土墩中埋葬墓葬最多的土墩。这次发掘充分说明，江南土墩墓不仅存在一墩一墓，而且存在一墩多墓，本次发掘资料显示，一墩多墓的现象明显较一墩一墓普遍。

明晰堆土掩埋与竖穴土坑共存

以往学术界普遍认为，作为先秦时期有别于其他地区的特殊葬俗的江南土墩墓一般没有墓坑，采用平地掩埋、平地起封的特殊方式安葬。后来也发现有土坑现象，但并不普遍。本次发掘的40座土墩共清理墓葬233座，绝大多数均有墓坑，同时在很多墓葬中还发现了人牙和人骨腐痕，这在中小土墩墓考古发掘中尚属首次，不仅从另一个方面佐证这些竖穴土坑就是墓葬，而且为江南地区青铜时代

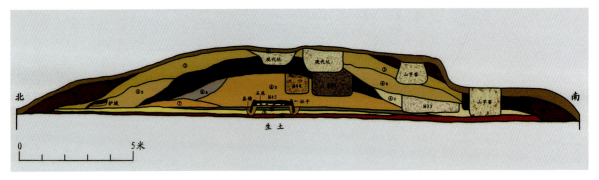

句容浮山果园29号墩南北向剖面图
Profile of North – South Section of Mound No. 29 at Guoyuan in Fushan, Jurong

句容浮山果园29号墩
Mound No. 29 at Guoyuan
in Fushan, Jurong

土著居民的人类学研究提供了宝贵的科学资料。堆土掩埋现象仅属个别，如浮山果园D29M41、许家沟D2M4。浮山果园D29M41就是堆土掩埋，平地起小封土，其中出土一组人牙。浮山果园D29M29、M42，浮山果园D27M2则是带浅坑和小封土的墓葬，为土墩墓中另一新的发现，它可能是我国发现的最早的带封土的墓葬。

首次发现一墩多墓的向心布局

发掘表明，一墩多墓土墩的墓葬布局方式多样，其中向心结构的布局方式较为特别，与中原及周边地区的墓地布局有着显著的差别，具有浓郁的江南土著特色，在土墩墓考古中也是首次发现。向心式布局即在土墩中心墓葬周围的不同层面安葬的多座墓葬头向均朝向中心墓葬。在40座土墩中有14座属于这种布局方式。

句容浮山果园29号墩M45石床墓门、柱洞
Posthole and Bed-shaped Stone Gate of Tomb M45 in Mound No. 29 at Guoyuan in Fushan, Jurong

句容浮山果园29号墩部分墓葬
Partial view of Tombs in Mound
No. 29 at Guoyuan in Fushan,
Jurong

句容寨花头2号墩鸟瞰
Top View of Mound No.2 at Zhaihuatou in Jurong

句容东边山1号墩M13（中间为船形棺，内有人骨朽痕）
Tomb M13 in Mound No.1 at Dongbianshan in Jurong
(boat-shaped coffin in the center with human bone relics)

发现形式多样的丧葬建筑

这次发掘的46座土墩中有9座墩子发现了14座丧葬建筑，包括墓上和墓下两种。

墓上建筑主要指在墩子中心墓葬上的建筑，由基槽、两面坡的棚子、石床等部分组成，有的还有通往墓葬的道路，在棚子上再堆土成丘。如东边山D2M1、浮山果园D29M45等。这类棚子建筑与浙江印山越王墓较为类似，而时代明显早于后者，级别低于后者，说明印山越王墓的丧葬建筑是有当时社会的丧葬习俗背景的。

墓下建筑是建在中心墓葬的下一层、墩子基础层面上的建筑物，同样包括基槽和柱洞。这类建筑一般位于墩子中心，建在中心墓葬的正下方，与中心墓葬没有直接关系，推测可能与营造墓地或墓葬的祭祀活动有关。如寨花头D5M8、寨花头D1M1。

首次发现明确的墓地界域

本次发掘中有1座土墩有明显的界墙和护坡，1座土墩有土垄，这在土墩墓发掘中为首次发现。句容东边山D1界墙平面近方形，营造于土墩的基础层面上，外侧有一周护坡，在西、南两面有两个缺口，土墩的堆积基本在界墙范围内，仅最上一层堆积局部溢出墙外。金坛薛埠上水

句容寨花头2号墩M22中心墓葬解剖一半情况
Cross-section of Tomb M22 at the Center of Mound No.2 at Zhaihuatou in Jurong

句容东边山4号墩M2祭祀遗迹
Offering Feature of Tomb M2 in Mound No.4 at Dongbianshan in Jurong

D4的土垄平面呈弧形，建造于生土面上，中部有一缺口，墩子的基础和各层堆积均在土垄范围内。从发掘情况看，界墙和土垄起到确定墓地四至的作用。在另两座土墩中发现护坡堆积，其功用可能与界墙、土垄相似。

没有明显界墙、土垄的土墩，其墓地的界域与墩子的基础范围大体一致，墩子堆积包括墓葬和祭祀器物群等活动基本在基础范围内，除最后覆土外，溢出现象未见。同时在墩子基础铺垫完后，墓地的范围也就确定了，尚未见改变墓地基础的现象。这些说明土墩作为墓地在建造之初就有了明确的规划。

还原土墩营造过程

土墩墓的发掘普遍采用四分法和探方法相结合。

从发掘的情况看，土墩的营造大致经历这样一个过程：首先平整土地；再在其上铺垫1至3层土，形成土墩的基础，现有资料显示基础完成，也就确定了墩子的范围，即确定了墓地的范围；在基础的中心部位建造中心墓葬及相关建筑，封土形成最早的坟丘。也有在土墩中部生土面或基础面上建造祭祀性建筑，后在建筑基础上堆土再建造中心墓葬；以后不同的时期在坟丘上堆土埋墓，或进行祭祀活动；在一定时期后再进行一次封土，停止埋墓和祭祀活动，完成该土墩即墓地的经营过程。

本次发掘的最大收获就是凭借考古层位学还原青铜时代江南土墩墓的营造过程及其社会面貌，并且在土墩墓的形制结构、丧葬习俗等诸多方面取得新的突破,不仅廓清了长期以来学术界对土墩墓的模糊认识,同时也为江南地区青铜时代的社会结构和土著文化,土墩墓的源流、分期与分区,以及土墩墓的保护和利用等重大课题的深入研究提供了翔实的第一手资料。

（供稿：林留根 王奇志 李虎仁 田名利）

Since the 1970s when the so called "Earth-Mound-Tombs" were first identified in southeast China, the debate over them has never stopped because of the extremely complicated structures of the earth mounds discovered in different places such as Jiangsu, Zhejiang and Shanghai.

In 2005, rescue excavations organized by the Museum of Nanjing along the alignments of the Ning - Chang and Zhen - Li Highways in Jurong County and Jintan County, Jiangsu Province, exposed 40 earth mounds, which yielded 233 tombs, 229 groups of ritual-utensil sets, and 14 tomb-architecture features. Over 3,800 artifacts with strong regional styles were unearthed, including mainly stoneware with geometric patterns and proto-porcelain. The 2005 excavation of the earth mounds tombs has greatly enriched cultural understanding of the Earth-Mound-Tombs, especially with regard to the arrangement and structure of the mound burials, as well as associated mortuary practice and ritual customs.

It is now confirmed that in addition to the arrangement of one mound for one tomb, there is also that of one mound for multiple tombs, and the latter is obviously more common. It was also verified that the practice of burying with earth co-existed with that of burying in vertical pits. It has been identified for the first time that multiple tombs within a mound were arranged in a circle and orientated towards the center of the mound. This type of burial arrangement presents a local characteristic that is unique to the areas south of the Changjiang (Yangtze) River. Furthermore, various types of tomb-architecture structures have been discovered, and demarcation features of the mound cemetery have been identified. Also verified through the excavation are the complicated ritual customs, e.g. the arrangement of funerary utensils into sets for offering.

原始青瓷罐
Proto-porcelain *guan*-jar

原始青瓷瓿
Proto-porcelain *bu*-jar

土墩墓出土器物
Artifacts Unearthed from Earth Mound Tombs

河南洛阳
东周车马坑及墓葬群

EASTERN ZHOU CHARIOT PITS AND TOMB
COMPLEX IN LUOYANG, HENAN

2005年,洛阳市文物工作队为配合基建工程,发掘了3座东周的车马坑及东周的墓葬群,发掘的地点属于东周王城遗址区。

此次共发掘了3座车马坑,编号为K19、K72、K73。

K19位于发掘区域的西部,长方形,南北向,长7.4、宽3、坑深1.53米。坑内由南向北依次放置5辆车。

1号车由车舆和车轮组成。两个车轮分置于车舆两侧,两轮内侧相距1.85米。东侧车轮直径1.27、西侧车轮横径1.36米,竖径1.34米。

车舆位于两轮之间,车厢由南向北倾斜,车舆北栏与两侧都压于土下,只露出前栏与车轼。从车舆南侧前栏推测,车厢东西宽1.35、前栏高31米。车轼与前栏上残留有红漆。

2号车与1号车结构相似。

3号车车舆东西宽1.63、南北长0.6米。车厢底部有数条桄木和横木,上铺席子。车厢上部东西向横置一根车轼。车厢中部有一柱状土包,与填土颜色不同,用途不详。

4号车最完整。车厢东西宽1.04、南北长0.59米,车厢只有东、南、西三侧车栏。车厢上部有车

车马坑K19全景
Full View of Chariot Pit K19

K19 马骨架
Horse Skeleton in K19

K19 4号车车厢底部席子
Straw Mat on Chamber Bottom of Chariot No.4 in K19

K19 5号车顶部伞盖
Canopy on Top of Chariot No.5 in K19

车马坑 K73 全景
Full View of Chariot Pit K73

清理 M12
Excavation at Tomb M12

M87 出土编钟
Bell-chimes from Tomb M87

墓葬出土带座铜方壶
Bronze Rectangular
hu-jar on Pedestal

墓葬出土铜簠
Bronze *fu*-container
Unearthed from Tomb

墓葬出土铜鼎
Bronze *ding*-tripod
Unearthed from Tomb

墓葬出土铜壶
Bronze *hu*-jar
Unearthed from Tomb

轼，由三条竖木支撑在车栏前。

车厢底部由几条桃木和横木支撑，上铺席子。

5号车顶部有完整的车伞盖，下部无法清理。伞盖长2.5、宽1.8米。变形较严重。

K73长7、宽2.86，坑深2.2米，马头向南。坑内共放置5辆车，所有的车轮都拆散后放置在坑的两壁。坑内填土为花土。

1号车由车舆和车辕组成，在车舆前部有一人头骨。

4号车上部保留了较完整的车伞盖。车厢无法清理。伞盖长2.2、宽1.36米。

K72近方形，长2.9、宽2.7米，坑内仅有两匹马，头向南。K72被后期的墓葬打破。

该工地共清理古墓98座，其中一座为汉墓，两座为秦墓。其余则为东周墓。东周墓皆为长方形竖穴土圹墓，长度在2.2～3.4米，宽度在1.2～2.8米之间，深在3～13米之间，属中小型墓葬。葬具多为一棺一椁。葬式多仰身直肢。未发现随葬品的墓有33座。出土铜礼器的墓有15座。仅出土玉蚌饰的墓有5座，其余的则以陶器为主要随葬品。

铜器的主要组合为：鼎、方壶、罍、簠、圆壶、盘、匜、舟、敦、戈、剑、镞以及车马器等，陶器的主要组合为：鼎、敦、壶，鼎、豆、壶，鼎、罐、豆、壶，鬲、盆、豆，鼎、敦、豆、壶，豆、罐等几种形式。从器形上分析，这批墓葬从春秋早期一直延续到战国晚期，乃至秦、汉。M93为规格最高的一座墓葬，出土了7个铜鼎和其他青铜礼器。它距K73最近，我们认为，K73应为M93的陪葬坑。M87出土了9个编钟及5个铜鼎，也是规格较高的一座墓葬。两座秦墓均为墓室略小于墓道的土洞墓。

在工地的东侧，有一条南北向的夯土墙。经发掘，夯土墙开口于①层下。宽约6米。夯土墙筑于生土之上。残留高度约1.6米。夯土墙是分段筑成的。在我们发掘的约30米范围内，夯土墙共有4段。经过解剖，初步断定这段夯土墙是东周时期的城墙。

（供稿：申建伟）

In 2005, as a mitigation measure for a construction project, the Archaeological Team of Luoyang City excavated three chariot pits and a cluster of tombs dated to the Eastern Zhou period. The excavated burial remains are located in Wangcheng, the capital city of the Eastern Zhou, in Luoyang City, Henan Province. K19 is a rectangular pit buried with five chariots lined up from south to north. Each chariot was composed of wheels and a chamber. At the chamber bottom of Chariot No.4, a piece of straw mat was found entirely preserved. At the top of Chariot No.5, a complete canopy remained intact.

K73 is also in a rectangular shape and buried with five chariots. The chariots were approximately arranged in the south-north direction and slightly piled up on each other. Besides, all the wheels were disassembled and then discarded in the pit; the chamber and hitch pole remained together.

K72 is smaller than the other two pits and buried with two horses.

All the excavated Eastern Zhou tombs are rectangular shaft pits. These tombs were either middle sized or small sized, mostly furnished with one coffin and one *guo*-out coffin. The bodies were mostly placed in an extended and supine position. The buried bronze set consisted of *ding*-tripod, rectangular *hu*-jar, *lei*-jar, *fu*-container, round hu-jar, *pan*-plate, and yi-ewer, among others. The pottery funerary vessels were combined in several ways, either in a set of *ding*-tripod, *dui*-container, and *hu*-jar, a set of *ding*-tripod, *dou*- plate on a pedestal, and *hu*-jar, a set of *ding*-tripod, *dou*-plate on a pedestal, and *guan*-jar, or a set of *li*-tripod, *pen*-basin, and dou-plate on a pedestal. Tomb M93 yielded seven bronze ding-tripods, presenting a relatively higher rank.

On the eastern side of the burial site, there is a stamped-earth wall which was aligned in the north-south direction and built section by section. The width of the wall is about 6 m and the remaining height 1.6m. After trenching, the wall is tentatively dated to the Eastern Zhou period.

夯土墙（由北向南）
Stamped-earth Wall (from north to south)

江苏无锡
鸿山越国贵族墓

ARISTOCRATIC TOMBS OF THE YUE STATE
AT HONGSHAN IN WUXI, JIANGSU

越国贵族墓地位于江苏省无锡市鸿山镇东部，这一地区现保存着大小规模的土墩近百座，分布于东西约6公里、南北约4公里的范围中。由于鸿山开发区的建设，部分土墩已受到工程建设的破坏。经国家文物局批准，2003年3月～2005年6月，南京博物院考古研究所和锡山区文物管理委员会组成考古队进行抢救性考古发掘。在开发区的范围内，共发掘了战国早期的越国贵族墓7座，根据土墩大小和墓葬规模，可分为小型、中型、大型和特大型墓。

小型墓2座，为长圆形馒首状土墩。其中邹家墩，长34.5、宽23.5、墩顶高出周围平地1.5米，平地起封，墓葬位于土墩近中部，墓坑长3.88、宽2.34、深0.35米，方向115°。随葬器物46件，青瓷器有盉、盅、器盖；硬陶器有瓿、钵、盅、器盖；夹砂陶器有甗和鼎；泥质陶器有鼎、罐、盆、器盖、璧、纺轮；玉器有管、璜、璧形佩、龙形佩和龟形佩；青铜器有环。

中型墓2座，为长方形覆斗状土墩。

其中的曹家坟，长35、宽26.9、高出周围平地2.9米，平地起封，墓葬位于土墩近中部，墓坑长8.75、宽2.25、深1.95米，方向110°。随葬器物93件，青瓷器有器盖；硬陶器有瓿、碗、盅；泥质陶器有盆、角形器、璧形器；玉器有璧形佩等。

大型墓2座。万家坟，为长方形覆斗状土墩。长47.4、宽38.8、高出周围平地3.8米，平地起封，墓葬位于土墩近中部，直接在表土上铺垫木料而构筑，垫木先纵铺三条东西向垫木，在垫木上再南北向横铺60余根稍有加工的木料，长16.68、宽5.07米，方向107°。该墓葬的特殊现象是在封土完成后，在墓室上方挖一纵向的长洞，然后在洞内进行焚烧，使墓室上方形成了厚达3米的红烧土。随葬器物519件，全部为陶器，主要置于墓葬的东部和西部，硬陶礼器有盉、盘、三足盘、炙炉、炉盘；硬陶乐器有甬钟、镈钟、磬、錞于、丁宁、句鑃、悬铃和鼓座，生活用品有瓿、罐、碗、钵、器盖等；泥质陶器有鼎、盆、匜和角形器、璧形器等。老虎墩的封土规模和平地铺木的葬制与万家坟同，但随葬品有玉瑗等玉器，成套的仿铜乐器中，不但有硬陶器，还有青瓷器。

特大型墓1座。丘承墩为长方形覆斗状土墩，原封土长68.2、宽40.6、以墓底计，封土高3.95米。墓葬位于土墩近中部，竖穴，深坑，平面呈"中"字形，由于土墩东部已被挖去，墓坑残长56.7米，方向110°，分为墓道、墓室和后室三部分，墓室内还用木板隔成主室和南、北侧室。墓道长21.2、宽3.65，墓室长23.6、宽6.3，后室长11.9、宽3.2，坑深3米。墓道南壁有长圆形壁龛，底部稍低于墓

丘承墩墓坑全景
Panoramic View of the Tomb Shaft in the
Qiucheng Mound

青瓷礼器出土情况
In-situ Celadon Ritual Utensils

道，长3.4、宽0.9、高0.5米。墓道中间有一条宽0.2米的排水沟，后室后还有长梯形斜坡状排水沟，沟长约12米。

该墓早年被盗，但出土随葬器物仍多达1098件，可分为青瓷器、陶器、玉器、琉璃器等。玉器和部分形体较大的青瓷器置于主室东部，青瓷角形器和璧形器置于主室中部，青瓷乐器主要置于壁龛中，而绝大多数随葬器物置于后室。其随葬器物数量之多，器类之齐全，器形之复杂，为江浙一带越国贵族墓之最。根据随葬器物的分布推测，墓主可能葬在墓室中部偏东，然由于被盗或埋葬环境等原

因，葬具和尸骨都已不存。

出土的青瓷器581件，大部分胎色灰白或局部泛红，釉色泛黄，脱釉严重；其中少量胎色泛白或灰白，釉色泛青，胎釉结合好，与常见的"原始青瓷"有着明显的差异。青瓷器主要为礼器、乐器和生活用品。其中礼器和生活用品441件，造型多仿青铜器。器类有盆形鼎、甑形鼎、豆、壶、三足壶、扁腹壶、罍、罐、匜、鉴、壶盆、三足盆、盘、三足盘、冰酒器、温酒器、盉、虎子、角形器、璧形器等。乐器140件，分10类，除磬为仿石、缶应为瓦器外，其余8类皆仿青铜器，其中既有仿中原系统的甬钟、镈钟和磬，亦有越系统的句鑃、丁宁、錞于、振铎、三足缶、悬鼓座和悬铃。

陶器472件，有瓿、罐、盆、角形器、璧形器和盘蛇玲珑球形器等。

玉器38件，可分为葬玉和佩玉。葬玉有覆面、带钩以及石璧；佩玉有龙形璜、龙凤璜、双龙首璜、云纹璜、龙首璜加觿组成的"五璜佩"，以及双龙佩和环形、璧形、削形、鞢形、管形、凤形、兔形佩饰。其中一件玉凤的纹饰用极细极浅阴刻，可能为最早的"微雕工艺"。此外还有琉璃璜、管、珠等。

鸿山越国贵族墓地中的墓葬，有一定的分布规律。特大型墓丘承墩位于墓地的西北角，

青瓷乐器出土情况
In-situ Celadon Musical Instruments

坐西朝东,而其他墓葬则以西面一座大型墓、东面一座中型墓、四周数座小型墓为一组,若干组墓葬围绕在丘承墩的东南至东北,呈扇形分布。

鸿山越国贵族墓的特征大致可归纳为:一、长方形覆斗状或长圆形封土;二、除特大型墓葬为"中"字形外,其余皆为长条形墓葬,墓葬皆东西向,大型墓的底部用垫木,特大型墓中墓室用木板相隔并有壁龛;三、随葬器物主要为原始青瓷器和硬陶器;四、特大型墓葬的随葬品中有成组的玉器;五、随葬器物中常见原始青瓷或硬陶的句鑃、錞于、丁宁、角形器、璧形器、悬铃等越系统的乐器以及越式鼎、筒形罐等越式礼器;六、高等级的器物纹样中常见越人的图腾——蛇。鸿山贵族墓地的墓葬形制以及随葬品的质地、器形、器类等均明显带有越国特征,应为越国墓葬;而随葬玉器、青瓷或硬陶的礼器、乐器,以及用蛇作为器物的常见装饰,表明鸿山一带应为一处重要的越国贵族墓地。

鸿山越国贵族墓地7座墓葬的随葬品中,皆有完全相同的器物,如麻布纹的瓮、罐,原始青瓷或

硬陶的钵、碗、盅、盖等,而大型和中型墓葬中还有造型完全相同的钟、镈、磬、悬铃、角形器、璧形器等,其年代亦应相同;而从陶器和青瓷器等生活用品的形态及器物的组合关系看,其年代应为战国早期;印纹硬陶的纹饰为麻布纹和米字纹,亦属战国早期的纹饰;出土玉器中,尽管有少量保留春秋晚期特征,而绝大多数都呈现战国早期的特征。因此鸿山越国贵族墓地的年代可定为战国早期,大致在公元前470年前后,即灭吴之后最强盛的越王勾践时代。

鸿山越国贵族墓地的发现是江浙地区在战国时期越国考古上的重要突破,其考古发掘的重要意义可归纳为:

一、由众多贵族墓葬所构成的越国贵族墓地在长江下游是首次发现,为系统研究越国史和越文化提供了科学而且丰富的考古资料。

二、鸿山贵族墓地的埋葬制度、等级制度和出土的成组成套的越国随葬品,可以系统地对越国的埋葬礼制、埋葬习俗和礼乐制度进行科学研究。

青瓷壶
Two Celadon *hu*-jars

青瓷罍
Celadon *Lei*-tripod

青瓷盉
Celadon *he*-pot

青瓷温酒器
Celadon Wine-warming Container

青瓷匜
F Celadon *yi*-ewer

青瓷甬钟
Celadon *yongzhong*-bells

青瓷悬铃
Celadon Hanging Bell

青瓷錞于和丁宁
Celadon *chunyu*-instru-
ments and *dingning*-bells

青瓷鼓座
Celadon Drum-base

青瓷鼓座
Celadon Drum-base

青瓷缶
Celadon *fou*-container

微雕羽纹凤形玉佩
Phoenix-shaped Jade Pendant
with Micro-carved Feature Design

四蛇四凤纹透雕玉带钩
Openwork Jade Belt-hook with Four-
snake and Four-Phoenix Design

透雕双龙纹玉管
Openwork Jade Tubes
with Double Dragon Design

浮雕盘蛇神兽纹玉管
Two Openwork Jade Tubes
with Coiling Snake Relief

浮雕纹饕餮玉鰈
Jade Archer's Thumb Ring
with *taotie* Relief

浮雕螭凤纹璧形玉佩
Disk-shaped Pendent with Feline
and Phoenix Relief

三、墓地出土的大批精美的越国玉器，为深入研究行越国玉器的制作工艺尤其是微雕工艺提供了实物资料。

四、鸿山越国贵族墓地成熟青瓷器的出土，更是研究和探讨我国瓷器的起源和发展的珍贵资料，首次发现的战国早期的低温琉璃釉陶器对于研究我国陶瓷史更是弥足珍贵。

五、鸿山越国贵族墓地出土的成套成组乐器，为研究中国音乐史和春秋战国时期越国乐器的组合、特征，提供了翔实的材料。

六、鸿山贵族墓地的完整性和随葬礼器、乐器的完整性，尤其是礼乐文化中和谐地融入中原礼制，对于越国礼乐制度与中原礼乐制度的相互关系的研究，乃至先秦史的综合研究，均有着积极和重要的意义。

（供稿：张 敏）

The aristocratic tombs at the Hongshan in Wuxi, Jiangsu Province, are the most important archaeological discovery of the Yue Culture after the excavation of the King's Mausoleum of the Yue State at Yinshan in Shaoxing, Zhejiang Province. In the aristocratic cemetery at Hongshan, archaeologists from the Museum of Nanjing excavated seven tombs and, based on the size and scale of the tombs and above earth mounds, classified the tombs into four categories: Super-large Tomb, Large Tomb, Middle Tomb, and Small Tomb. Over 1,000 funeral objects were unearthed from Super-large tombs, including celadon ritual utensils, musical instruments, and Jade items. The objects from the Super-large tombs are the highest-ranked funerary goods so far found from the Yue State. Therefore, the excavation of aristocratic tombs at Hongshan is highly significant for the study of a series of academic subjects, e.g. the rite-and-music system of the Yue State during the Spring and Autumn period, the origin of celadon porcelain, and the technique of jade micro-carving.

河南内黄
三杨庄汉代田宅遗存

HAN FARM - MANSION SITE
AT SANYANGZHUANG IN NEIHUANG, HENAN

三杨庄汉代遗址位于河南省内黄县南部梁庄镇
三杨庄北，地处黄河故道，因当地实施硝河
疏浚工程，2003年6月，在三杨庄村北河道范围内
发现了4处汉代瓦顶建筑遗存。河南省文物考古研
究所于2003年7月~12月对其中的西部两处遗存
进行了部分清理，确认这些遗存为汉代宅院建筑遗
址，因黄河的一次大规模洪水泛滥而被整体淹没。
2005年初，又发现了两处宅院遗存及部分汉代墓
葬。2005年3~12月，在国家文物局的直接支持下，
河南省文物部门又对这两处遗存进行了发掘清理。
两次清理面积总计约9000平方米，迄今只是对这
四处宅院遗存的坍塌原貌进行了平面揭露，尚未作
单体或局部解剖工作。

　　第一处宅院建筑遗存位于三杨庄村北约500
米。本区域目前勘探面积3600平方米。在钻探范
围内，南、北部均发现有较大面积的夯土遗存，南
部发现有古道路遗迹，宽约4米。这些遗迹均位于
同一地层深度，距现地表深5米左右。

　　在本区域内，对已暴露于河道内的宅院遗存部
分进行了初步发掘清理，清理面积400余平方米。
清理出的遗迹有宅院围墙、正房的瓦屋顶、墙体砖
基础、坍塌的夯土墙、未使用的板瓦和筒瓦、建筑
废弃物堆积、拌泥池、灶、灰炕等。出土有轮盘、
盆、瓮等陶器。从已清理部分的情况看，应当为整

座宅院的第二进院落的一部分，其中有一部分尚未
使用的板瓦、筒瓦仍被整齐地叠摞在天井内。结合
主房东北侧有一堆筒板瓦碎块，西南侧有一小的拌
泥池，故推测，主房正在维修过程中洪水来临，维
修工作没能完成。由于洪水过后这里成了黄河河道
的一部分，所以，维修时的原状得以保存下来。

　　第二处宅院遗存位于三杨庄村西北，东距第一
处宅院遗存约500米，该处宅院遗址揭露较为完整，
遗址总面积近2000平方米。宅院的平面布局从南
向北依次为：第一进院南墙及南大门、东厢房、西
门房，第二进院南墙、南门、西厢房、正房等。南
大门外偏东南约5米处还有一眼水井及通往水井的
用碎瓦铺设的便道，水井壁系小砖圈砌，井口周围
用同样的砖铺砌成近方形的低井台；水井的周围还
分布有较多的水槽、盆、瓮等陶器和石磨等；水井
西侧约5米处，有一处特殊的编织遗存，遗迹四角
为三块砖摞成的四个分布呈长方形的砖垛，砖垛内
堆积有较多的长宽为10×5厘米的砖块，砖块的中
部刻有可以缠线的凹槽，故此，推测该处可能为编
制竹席或草席类物品的遗迹。宅院西北角有一带瓦
顶的厕所。在宅院的西侧，还清理出一座形状规范
的圆形水池。在该宅院遗址内及南大门外、水池内，
清理出5个大石臼、2个小石臼、石磨、石碾等以
及水槽、碗、甑、盆、罐、豆、瓮、轮盘等陶器，

第一处庭院东侧堆放的尚未使用的
板瓦、筒瓦（由东北向西南）
Unused Segmental Tiles and
Semi-cylindrical Tiles Piled on
Eastern Side of Mansion No.1
(from northeast to southwest)

第一处庭院主房内出土的陶轮盘（正面）
Front View of Potter's Wheel Unearthed
from Main House in Mansion No.1

第一处庭院主房内出土的陶轮盘（背面）
Back View of Potter's Wheel Unearthed
from Main House in Mansion No.1

还有犁、釜、刀等铁器；主房瓦顶东侧表层清理出带有"益寿万岁"字样瓦当的筒瓦数件；二进院内西部地面初步清出 3 枚"货泉"铜钱等。

第三处宅院建筑遗存位于三杨庄村北，东北距第一处宅院遗存近 100 米。该宅院建筑遗存揭露得也较为完整，面积大致为 30×30 平方米，宅院的平面布局从南向北依次为：第一进院南墙及南大门、南厢房，第二进院墙、正房等，宅院四周有院墙。宅院东西墙外分别有一条宽窄、长度大致相同的水沟，西侧水沟分为南北两段。南门外西侧有水井一眼，井壁的用砖及砌法与第二处宅院的水井相同，只是没有砖铺的井台。宅院后有一小的建筑遗存，目前推测可能为厕所。正房后还发现有两排树木残存遗迹，从清理出的残存的树叶痕迹初步判断多为桑树，也有榆树。南厢房版筑夯土南墙的块状大小清晰可辨。特别是在该宅院的东西两侧水沟外和后面（北侧）清理出有排列整齐、高低相间的田垄遗迹，田垄的宽度大致在 60 厘米左右。有迹象表明，在南门外不大的活动场地南侧，也为农田，且有一条不宽的南北向与外界相通的道路。在宅院内外的地面上散落有石碓、小石臼、陶瓮、陶盆等遗物，同时还发现有半枚"货泉"铜钱。

第四处宅院建筑遗存位于第三处宅院遗存东25 米，大致东西并列，尚未完整清理与揭露。平面

第二处庭院全景（由南向北）
Panoramic View of Mansion
No.2 (from south to north)

第二处庭院东厢房瓦顶保存情况
（由北向南）
Tiled Roof of Eastern Side
House in Mansion No.2 (from
north to south)

布局接近第三处宅院遗存。

从目前已清理的四处宅院的情况看，其均为坐北朝南；均为二进院布局，南门外为小范围的活动场地，且各自有水井；宅院之间互不相连，四周由农田相隔；所有房屋顶部均使用有瓦，主房屋顶更是全部用瓦。综合已知初步判断，这是一处属西汉晚期的大规模的聚落遗址。其是否为一处汉代的村落（闾里）或城镇，大的布局如何等情况，尚有待进一步的考古勘探和发掘才能确定。该遗址因黄河的某一次（结合《汉书》有关记载，推测为新莽时期）大规模泛滥而被淤沙淹没深埋，因而，整个聚落遗址内的各类遗迹现象，能够得以原貌保存，这为目前全国汉代考古所仅见。

无疑，三杨庄汉代聚落遗址具有多学科特别丰富的信息和重大的研究价值。当然，目前的发现和考古及研究工作仅仅是初步的，下一步的考古工作正在规划之中。

（供稿：刘海旺 朱汝生）

第二处庭院第一进院内出土石磨
Stone Mill unearthed from First Yard
in Mansion No.2

第二处庭院出土石臼
Stone Mortar unearthed
from Mansion No.2

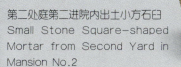

第二处庭第二进院内出土小方石臼
Small Stone Square-shaped
Mortar from Second Yard in
Mansion No.2

第二处庭院主房瓦顶使用的
瓦当
Tile Ends on Roof of
Main House in Mansion
No.2

第三处庭院西侧田垄正在清理之中（由西北向东南）
Exposed Field Ridges West of Mansion No.3
(from northwest to southeast)

第三处庭院全景（由北向南）
Panoramic View of Mansion
No.3 (from north to south)

第三处庭院主房瓦顶北半部分保存状况（由西向东）
Condition of Northern Part of Tiled Roof on Main House in Mansion No.3 (from west to east)

第三处庭院主房瓦顶北半部分保存状况（由北向南）
Condition of Northern Part of Tiled Roof on Main House in Mansion No.3 (from north to south)

第三处庭院（右）与第四处宅院之间的田垄遗迹（由东北向西南）
Remains of Field Ridges between Mansion No.3 (right) and Mansion No.4 (from northeast to southwest)

In the summer of 2003, a well preserved site of the Han period was discovered in the old water course of the Yellow River in Neihuang County, Henan Province. Through excavations from June 2003 to December 2005 conducted by the Henan Provincial Institute of Archaeology, it is primarily confirmed that this site is a well preserved settlement of the Han period which was deeply covered by silty sand due to the flooding of the Yellow River. On this large site, seven mansions or house complexes were identified and four of them primarily exposed. The major discoveries include mansion yards, tiled roofs of houses, in-situ collapsed walls, remaining features and artifacts of various types in the yards as well as farm fields outside the mansions. The Sanyangzhuang site is the first unearthed farm-mansion site of the Han period. The excavation at Sanyangzhuang, therefore, is a brand new archaeological discovery of the Han agricultural civilization.

甘肃礼县鸾亭山汉代祭祀遗址

LUANTINGSHAN SITE IN LIXIAN, GANSU

礼县鸾亭山遗址位于甘肃省礼县县城西北的山顶上，属于黄土峁梁地貌，山势极陡，海拔1700米，面积2000平方米。2004年由甘肃省文物考古研究所、北京大学考古文博学院、中国国家博物馆田野考古部、陕西省考古研究所、西北大学文博学院考古系组成的早期秦文化联合考古队对该遗址进行了调查和钻探，并于2004、2005年两次进行了发掘。

遗址地面有大量残瓦片、兽骨，遗址西北角残存有2米高的夯土台。两次共发掘面积1600平方米，钻探3000平方米，发现灰坑28个、祭祀坑1个、犬祭坑1个、灶2个、房址6座、沟4个、围墙1道，出土玉器、骨器、瓦当70余件（组）和大量的陶片、瓦片。

遗址包括上部的圆坛和下部的平台两部分，圆坛周围有汉代夯土墙，厚0.7~1.2米，夯土紧密，其下有基槽，基槽宽约2.75米，围墙东部内侧有柱洞。除西部、西北部的2座汉代房址、5个灰坑、2个圆形的灶外，其余遗迹均在圆坛下、夯土墙内。

灰坑平面多为圆形，也有部分方形、椭圆形，口径0.5~2.5米，主要分布在北部偏东以及东部和西南部。以汉代的居多，多分布在北部、中部，而周代的灰坑主要在西南和东部，其中发现有周代灰坑叠压寺洼灰坑的现象。

在平台近围墙的缺口处有一个祭祀坑，编号为K1，圆角方形，深2.8米，内埋丰富的兽骨。兽骨分层埋葬，自上而下连续堆积，均被肢解，个体有几十个。可辨种类有牛、羊、猪、鹿、狗及禽类的骨骼。

犬祭坑在北部汉代浅沟东部，葬一完整的狗，坑内有零星汉代陶片。

房址主要分布在西南、西北和中部，均为方形，其中周代的2座，汉代的4座。周代的房址在西南、西北，均为地面建筑，长方形。汉代的房址集中在中部，长方形，有墙。

沟4条，其中南部3条，北部1条，均为长条形，宽1~4、长4~30米。其中南北向2条，东西向2条。

整个遗址中，周代的遗迹主要分布在南部，发现有西周时期的灰坑和房子；汉代的遗迹主要集中在北部，包括灰坑、房址、灰沟等。出土了大量"长乐未央"瓦当及筒瓦、板瓦等，瓦当时代多为汉中期，筒瓦、板瓦为汉中晚期。板瓦上的纹饰有方格纹、菱形纹、布纹、绳纹、划纹等近10种。

遗址俯瞰
Top View of the Site

在遗址北部编号为G4长约20米的东西向汉代半月形浅沟内，清理出土了11套组合完整的玉器，玉器的总数则超过50件；器类有圭、璧、玉人三种。组合方式有圭压璧的，有璧压圭的，也有多件玉璧上下叠压的。玉圭直径4.4～16厘米，最大者长约16、宽约7厘米。玉璧直径12～22厘米。部分圭、璧上有朱砂痕迹。圭多青玉，璧多白玉。另有玉人2件，一男一女，与圭、璧共出。浅沟南、北两侧内有柱洞。

在鸾亭山的山腰位置还有两处东西对称的夯土

犬祭坑
Dog-sacrifice Pit

柱洞
Postholes

玉器出土情况
Jades in Exposure

玉器出土情况
Jades in Exposure

"长乐未央"瓦当
Tile-end with "*changle weiyang*" characters

台,西台被破坏严重,东台有上、下二级,貌似"子母阙"。夯土台所处的山梁上为周代墓葬区,遭严重盗掘,地表有马骨,疑为马坑所出。山腰和山顶的建筑遗迹应该构成了一组完整的祭祀区,山顶的祭祀遗址和山腰的夯土建筑应有内在联系,这也是将来工作需要解决的问题。

通过发掘可知,鸾亭山在周代就有人类居住、活动,到了汉代则成为专门的祭祀场所。出土的50余件玉器绝大多数为圭或璧,结合遗址的布局结构和所处的地形环境,初步推断它是一处汉代的祭天场所,而汉代祭祀用玉的发现,为了解相关礼制提供了重要的考古学资料。

（供稿：李永宁）

玉人
Jade Human Figurine

3件玉器成组出土
Three Jades Clustered in Exposure

玉器表面有朱砂痕迹
Jades with Cinnabar Traces on Surface

出土时玉圭叠压玉璧
Jade *gui*-scepters on top of Jade *bi*-disks in Exposure

玉璧
Jade *bi*-disk

玉璧
Jade *bi*-disk

The Luantingshan site is located northwest of the town seat of Lixian County, Gansu Province. The site is situated on a hilltop and surrounded by a moat in three directions, and the remaining open side is connected to a deep valley. As a sacrificial site with a size of approximately 2,000 sq m, the Luantingshan site consists of two components: the upper round altar and the lower platform. The round altar is surrounded along its edge by a stamped-earth wall built on the ground level during the Han period. Based on the postholes identified on the inner side of the wall, there were probably corridor-like structures on the altar during the Han time.

During 2004 and 2005, a joint archaeological team was organized by the Gansu Provincial Institute of Archaeology, Beijing (Peking) University, The National Museum of China, the Shaanxi Provincial Institute of Archaeology, and the Northwest University. The joint team conducted excavations in two field seasons. The team identified features dated to the Siwa Culture period, the Zhou period, and the Han period, including stamped-earth walls, house foundations, sacrificial pits, a dog-sacrifice pit, fire stoves, and ditches. Over 70 pieces (or sets) of artifacts were unearthed, including bronze, pottery, stone, and jade objects, and large amounts of tile-ends with "*changle weiyang*" characters as well as semi-cylindrical and segmented tiles. It is especially remarkable that over 50 jades were unearthed from a half-moon shaped shallow ditch in the east-west direction. These jades were grouped in 11 clusters, including human figurines, *bi*-disks, and *gui*-scepters. The excavations demonstrate that the Luantingshan site should theoretically be a sacrificial temple to heaven. This site therefore provides important archaeological data for the study of associated ritual systems.

东西两座夯土台
Two Stamped-earth Platforms
in the East and West Directions

山东胶州赵家庄汉代墓地的发掘

EXCAVATION OF THE HAN CEMETERY AT ZHAOJIAZHUANG IN JIAOZHOU, SHANDONG

赵家庄墓地位于山东省胶州市里岔镇赵家庄村东南，现为青岛市市级文物保护单位。整个墓地坐落在岭地上，地表有大小不等的封土14座，封土台基的形状多呈圆角方形或椭圆形，面积150～2000平方米不等。

2005年5～6月，为配合青岛至莱芜高速公路工程建设，山东省文物考古研究所、青岛市文物局、胶州市博物馆组成联合考古队，对赵家庄墓地进行了抢救性考古发掘。发掘采用在封土台基上开挖多条平行探沟的方式，充分利用探沟的平剖面进行分析研究，初步搞清了封土墓的结构、堆筑方式、形成过程和墓穴布局和数量。共发掘7座封土，分别为1～3、5～8号。清理墓葬73座，出土瓷、陶、铜、玉、漆木器等珍贵文物约350件。

土墩墓的构筑方式和形成过程大致分两种类型，一类是先在岭地上堆筑一台基，然后在台基上修墓并堆筑封土，之后再以台基一侧或周缘为依托，不断扩大台基并挖筑墓穴，逐渐形成更大的封土。另类封土的形成过程是，先在岭地上择地开挖墓穴埋葬死者，在其上一次性堆筑较大的封土台基，然后在其上顺次修墓并埋葬死者。这类封土台基以后的发展过程和第一类基本相同，即等封土台基上的墓穴达到一定数量后，再顺台基一侧或周缘添筑封土，并修建墓穴。

墓地中的每座封土是一个相对独立的墓区。1号、3号封土台基周围存在界沟。每座封土中有1个或多个墓穴，墓穴的数量与封土面积大致成正比。清理的73座小型墓，其中32座出自5号土墩。单座封土内的墓葬布局有一定的规律，排列有序，多成组或成排分布。少量墓葬存在打破关系，具有

9号土墩全景
Panoramic View of Mound No.9

2号土墩墓穴分布状况
Distribution of Grave Pits on Mound No.2

打破关系的每组墓的墓向基本一致,前者多打破后者的一侧边。

以1号封土为例,介绍封土墓的封土结构和墓穴埋葬特点。该封土平面大致呈梯形,东窄西宽。东端地势最高,仍保留有圆锥形封土堆。中西部则呈斜坡状。面积约1200余平方米。环封土台基东、北、南侧有一条界沟,宽2.5～3.5、深0.46～1米。沟斜壁内收、圆底,顺地势由东向西有逐渐加深的趋势。土墩依地势而筑,堆积由东向西大致分三部分。一部分的土层栽种大致呈水平状平铺叠压堆筑,土质、土色、包含物和结构也差别较大;局部堆积分层较多,平铺或坡状叠压堆筑而成。后两期堆筑的封土是在一期封土基础上略加修整,依附西面坡由东向西叠压扩建而成,呈坡状堆积。封土台基中共发现13座墓,其中打破一期封土的墓有4座,打破二期封土的墓有3座,打破三期封土的墓6座。部分墓葬成组分布,如M3和M10、M6和M13、M7和M12等。

土墩中的墓穴为长方形竖穴土坑或岩坑。墓穴长2.8～4.6、宽1.1～2米,个别墓葬近方形,边

长4米左右。葬具为木质棺椁,多为一棺,部分墓葬一棺一椁,椁室为木质 "井"字形结构。棺外髹黑漆,内髹红漆。部分墓葬存在器物箱,有头箱和边箱之分。器物箱均为木质,单独放置。1号和5号封土中还发现少量砖椁墓,墓穴内有长方形弧壁或直壁砖椁,墓砖在朝向墓室的侧面模制菱形纹、钱币纹图案。墓主骨架腐蚀严重,葬式可辨者均仰身直肢,头向大都朝向东南;6号封土中的7座墓与其他墓葬不同,头向东北。绝大多数墓葬中有随葬品,数量1～17件不等。随葬品中的陶瓷容器,车马器基本上都放在器物箱内或棺外,化妆用具和小饰件等则放在棺内或墓主人身上。铜镜多盛于漆盒中,放在墓主人头侧。

出土遗物丰富,有原始瓷、釉陶、陶、铜、铁、玉石、木器、漆器等。陶瓷器164件。原始瓷器中有壶、罐,其中壶有喇叭口和盘口之分,有的肩部施以对称双耳。釉陶器数量较少,均为壶。原始瓷器和釉陶器上饰有弦纹、刻划纹、水波纹和凤鸟纹等。陶器有壶、罐、瓮等。铜器有舟、盆、镜、带钩、环、印章、车马饰件(铜泡、马镳等)、铺首

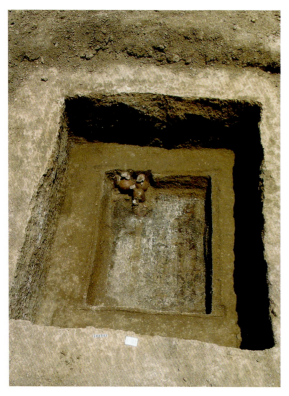

1号土墩M4
Tomb M4 on Mound No. 1

5号土墩M6
Tomb M6 on Mound No. 5

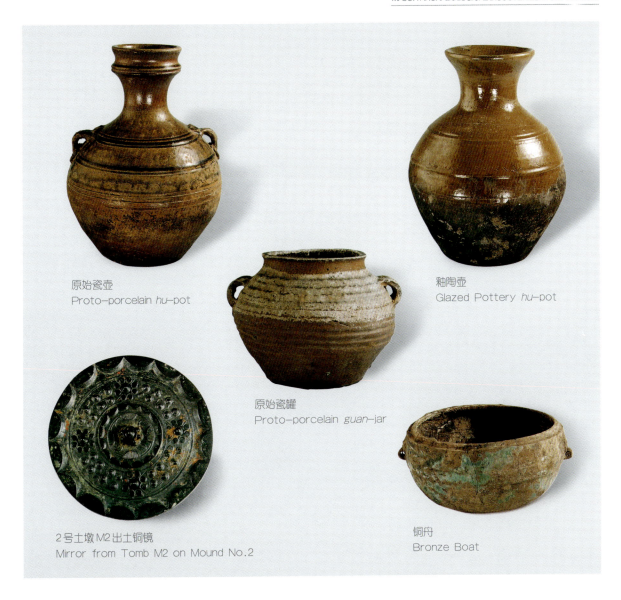

原始瓷壶
Proto-porcelain *hu*-pot

釉陶壶
Glazed Pottery *hu*-pot

原始瓷罐
Proto-porcelain *guan*-jar

2号土墩 M2 出土铜镜
Mirror from Tomb M2 on Mound No.2

铜舟
Bronze Boat

和铜钱等，部分饰件鎏金。铜镜数量较多，共出土约30面，有昭明镜、日光镜、百乳镜、草叶纹镜、蟠螭纹镜、星云纹镜、七乳四神禽兽镜等。印章为汉代常见的鼻纽印，印面约1.7厘米见方。铁器有铁削等。玉石器有璧、环、蝉、黛板等。木器有梳、篦、束发器等。漆器有奁、盒等。

根据墓葬结构和随葬品特征分析，墓葬年代主要集中在两汉时期，个别墓葬延续至魏晋。墓地墓葬封土规模较大，随葬品丰富，昭示出墓葬主人具有一定经济实力和社会地位。每座封土可能就是一个家族墓地，不同的封土墓分属不同的家族。5号封土M18出土的1枚铜印章，印文为"王何之印"，据此判断该封土墓可能为王姓家族所建。墓地距赵家庄西北约4公里处为汉代被国故城，推测墓地和该故城有一定的关系。

墓葬中原始瓷器的种类、形态、釉色和胎质和江浙一带发现的同类器相近，因此山东境内汉代原始瓷有可能来自江浙一带。

这类汉代封土墓大量存在于山东鲁东南地区，具有一定的地域特点。已经发掘的同类封土墓还有日照市海曲、胶南市河头、沂南县宋家哨等墓地。赵家庄墓地的发掘，规模较大，基本搞清了这类汉代封土墓的结构和埋葬特点，为深入研究山东地区汉代丧葬制度提供了重要的实物资料。

（供稿：兰玉富 李文胜 王磊）

113

铜印章
Bronze Seal

铜印章印文
Inscriptions on Bronze Seal

During May and June 2005, the Shandong Provincial Institute of Archaeology carried out a rescue excavation at the Zhaojiazhuang cemetery in Jiaozhou of Shandong, opening seven earth mounds, excavating 73 tombs, and yielding over 350 precious relics.

A preliminary understanding has been reached on the boundary and distribution of the cemetery, on the structure of the mound-burials, and on the arrangement of the tombs. The construction of mound burials was a continued expanding process: a mound was first piled up on the hill, then a grave shaft was dug into the mound; afterwards, additional mounds were built up lying on the original mound, together composing a much larger mound. Every mound in the cemetery was a relatively independent subdivision, and boundary ditches were found surrounding platforms of some mounds. Every mound contained one or multiple graves, which were arranged following certain rules or patterns, either grouped or lined up. The shafts of the tombs were rectangular earth pits or rock pits. The tomb furniture included a wooden *guan*-coffin and a *guo*-out coffin. There were also storage boxes in some tombs. The occupants of the tombs were mostly arranged with their heads towards the southeast, and most of the tombs were buried with funerary goods. The unearthed rich remains consisted of wares of various kinds, including proto-porcelain, glazed pottery, pottery, bronze, iron, jade, stone, wood and lacquer.

The tombs discovered at the Zhaojiazhuang cemetery are mostly dated to the Western Han and Eastern Han, with some exceptions dated to the later Wei and Jin periods. It is now assumed that different mounds probably belong to different families. Mound burials of this kind are very common in southeast Shandong, representing a certain regional characteristic. The excavation of the Zhaojiazhuang cemetery, therefore, has provided important material evidence for the further study of the funerary system of the Han dynasties in the Shandong area.

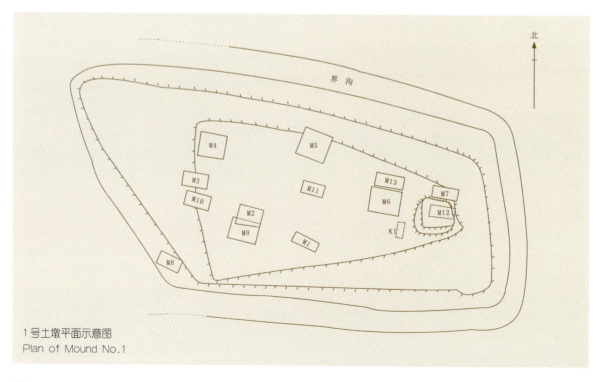

1号土墩平面示意图
Plan of Mound No.1

山西大同
沙岭北魏壁画墓

NORTHERN WEI MURAL TOMB AT SHALING, DATONG, SHANXI

墓葬区位于大同市御河之东、沙岭村东北约1公里的高地上。2005年7月12日接到群众举报后,大同市考古研究所立即对这个已经暴露出古代墓葬的取土场进行了勘探,经国家文物局批准,对发现的12座北魏时期墓葬进行了抢救性发掘,出土文物200余件,其中M7保存有精美壁画和文字题记。

M7为长斜坡墓道砖构单室墓,由墓道、甬道、墓室三部分组成,方向272°。墓道残长10、宽1.2～1.4米。墓道与甬道相接处有砖砌的封门墙,甬道拱券顶,长1.6、宽1.14、高1.8米,地砖呈人字形铺设与墓室相连。墓室位于甬道的东端,平面呈弧边长方形,东西最长处3.45米,南北最宽处2.9米,墓室的高度残留2.14米。墓顶上部早已破坏,根据现状判断应为四角攒尖顶。全墓以长28、宽14、厚5厘米的灰砖砌筑,用黄泥粘接。墓室内盗扰破坏严重,回填土中有许多木质碎渣,棺底有大量的木炭,用以防潮。在墓室的西北角存有北魏墓中惯用的石灰枕,但未见人骨架。只是在墓室的东部发现了两段牛腿骨。出土器物共27件,有铜牌饰1件、铜帐钩1件、银圆饰6件、铜泡钉1件、铁器1件、釉陶壶5件、素陶壶5件、素陶罐6件,还有一件残漆耳杯,底部依稀可见"莫人"2个刻划文字。

墓中出土了大量的彩绘漆片,色泽鲜艳亮丽,画面清晰。

M7墓室
Chamber of Tomb M7

115

出土釉陶壶
Glazed Pottery *hu*-Pot

出土漆耳杯
Lacquer Cup

出土铜泡钉
Bronze Round Nail

经过初步拼对，可知有男女主人端坐、庖厨、扬场等生活场面。身着鲜卑服的男主人怀拥凭几、手持龙扇端坐于围屏内的榻上，面前摆放着曲足案，上有一圆形食盒，案下有外黑内红的漆耳杯。

在一大块的漆片上有墨书文字 3 行，约百余字，可辨识部分的文字为："□□□□元年岁次豕韦月建中吕廿一日丁未侍中主客尚书领太子少保平西大将军破多罗太夫人□□□□殡于弟宅迄于仲秋八月将祔葬□□□于殡宫易以□□□慈祥之永住□□□□无期□□之德昊天冈极□莫□□哀哉□岁月云"。虽有文字题记，但在纪年的关键处缺字。据《广雅·释天》"营室谓之豕韦"可知，豕韦指的是二十八宿中的营室，亦即室宿。而营室与十二次的关系，据《汉书·律历志》，其在十二次的"诹訾"中。《左传·襄公三十年》孔颖达正义

曰："十二次，子为弦枵，亥为诹訾。"那么题记中"岁次豕韦"应是地支为"亥"之年。中吕是古乐十二律的第六律，其于十二月为四月，因亦用以称农历四月。北魏时期，合乎"元年"、"四月"和"二

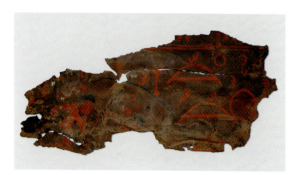

漆画残片（扬场）
Scene of Winnowing on Matched Lacquer Pieces

漆画残片（墨书文字）
Ink Inscriptions on Matched Lacquer Piece

漆画残片（人物）
Human Figures on Matched
Lacquer Pieces

漆画残片（庖厨）
Scene of Cooking on
Matched Lacquer Pieces

十一日丁未"3个条件的，仅有太武帝太延元年。是年为公元435年，干支纪年为乙亥，也符合"亥为諏訾"之说，合于"岁次豕韦"的条件。是故题记漶灭之处，应是"太延"2字。也就是说，墓主人卒于太延元年农历四月二十一日。破多罗氏为鲜卑人，其任侍中、平西大将军等职，他的母亲死后与其先逝的父亲于仲秋八月合葬。

壁画分布在墓室四壁和甬道的顶、侧部，保存基本完整，总面积约24平方米。壁画绘于砖壁外的白灰层上，先用红线勾画轮廓大体定位，再以黑线定稿，然后着色，设色基本为红、黑、孔雀蓝、绿四种颜色。壁画的线条流畅自然，风格雄劲奔放。

北壁壁画分上下两栏，上栏绘奇禽异兽，下栏绘车马出行。车马出行场面宏大，人物众多，从上到下共排列7行，分别绘有列队的侍女、导骑、骑乐、仪仗等，队伍中间是一辆高大华丽的车。东壁正中绘一高大的建筑物，庑殿顶，鸱尾上翘，顶中间站立一只金翅鸟。建筑内挂有帷幔，里面端坐男女二人，应是墓主人夫妇。建筑物的周围有车辆、马匹、人物等，两侧各有一棵枝繁叶茂的大树。南壁的主要画面内容为宴饮和庖厨。围隔的步障弯弯曲曲，将场景分为两部分。东面有居住的房屋和数量较多的乐伎、侍仆、食物、酒具以及马匹，是一幅场面较大的群宴图。西面有粮仓、装满货物的架

墓室北壁壁画全景
Panoramic View
of North-wall
Paintings
in Chamber

墓室北壁壁画局部（出行）
Scene of Chariot Procession on North-wall of Chamber

墓室北壁壁画局部（神兽）
Mysterious Animal Depicted
on North Wall of Chamber

墓室北壁壁画局部（神兽）
Mysterious Animal Depicted
on North Wall of Chamber

子车、红顶卷棚车以及4个顶部可以开启的毡帐。大的毡帐中有端坐和站立的女性，她们的周围放有许多食物和温酒樽等生活用具，前面还有持物忙碌的侍仆和伴奏表演的乐伎。另外还有杀羊、烤羊肉串和酿酒等场面。

西壁在甬道两侧，红边作框各有一个双腿分开站立、单手高举盾牌的武士。甬道顶部则绘汉晋时期常见的伏羲女娲神话题材。画面上两人头戴花冠，眉目清秀，下半截龙身交缠在一起。

M7既有色彩亮丽的漆画又有保存基本完整的壁画，还有墨书的纪年文字，这在已发现的北魏平城时期的众多墓葬中是仅见的，这是我国魏晋南北朝时期重要的田野考古发现。M7绘画中有出行、宴饮、百戏、酿酒、杀羊、扬场、怪兽等内容，展现的是墓主人生活时代——北魏太延年间的社会现实生活，从形象和风格来看，其更接近于汉魏。墓葬主人虽然是鲜卑人，但是绘画内容清楚地展现了少数民族统治的北方地区当时汉化的程度。

（供稿：刘俊喜）

墓室东壁壁画全景
Panoramic View of East-wall Paintings in Chamber

墓室南壁壁画全景
Panoramic View of South-wall Paintings in Chamber

甬道顶部壁画（伏羲、女娲）
Fu Xi and Nv Wa Painted on Ceiling of Passage

甬道北侧壁画局部（武士）
Warrior Painted on North Side of Passage

墓室西壁壁画（武士）
Warrior Depicted on West Wall of Chamber

甬道南侧壁画
Wall Paintings on South Side of Passage

甬道北侧壁画
Wall Paintings on North Side of Passage

The tomb is located in a cemetery which lies on the terrace approximately 1 km northeast of Shaling village, which is east of the Yuhe River in Datong. Within the cemetery, 12 tombs have been excavated but a single-chamber brick tomb M7 is the only one with preserved murals.

Tomb M7 was orientated in the east-west direction and composed of a long sloping tunnel, a vaulted passage, and a chamber yielding 27 artifacts. The matching of the remaining lacquer pieces from the tomb resulted in the discovery of colored paintings and written inscriptions. The lacquer paintings consisted of scenes of the tomb occupant seated, cooking, and spade-waving. According to the inscriptions, the occupant of Tomb M7 was the mother of a high ranking Xianbei (xienpi) official, General Poduoluo, and she died in the first year of the Taiyan Reign (AD 435) of Emperor Taiwu of the Northern Wai dynasty. The wall paintings were found on the entire four walls of the chamber and the ceiling of the passage, with a total size of 24 sq m. The contents of the paintings included a chariot procession, sitting male and female hosts, banqueting, warriors, the legendary god Fu Xi and goddess Nu Wa, and mysterious animals of various types. The images were depicted with simple and smooth lines, showing a bold and forceful style.

Among all the graves dated to the Pinching period (398 - 493) of the Northern Wei, Tomb M7 is the only one clearly dated with a confirmed tomb occupant and rich burial remains. Therefore, it is highly valuable for academic and artistic studies.

西安北郊北周李诞墓

NORTHERN WEI TOMB OF LI DAN IN NORTHERN SUBURB OF XI'AN, SHAANXI

李诞墓位于西安市北郊南康村，南距坑底寨北周康业墓约 500 米、安伽墓约 650 米，东距井上村北周史君墓约 2000 米。2005 年 9 月，西安市文物保护考古所对该墓进行了抢救性发掘。

该墓形制为长斜坡墓道穹隆顶砖室墓，平面呈"甲"字形，坐北朝南，方向 180°，由墓道、甬道和墓室三部分组成。甬道中部立一扇石门，石门外侧置墓志一合。

墓室平面方形略外弧，穹隆顶，东西长 3.62~3.88、南北宽 3.56~3.65、高 3.74 米。墓室四壁先抹一层泥，然后涂较薄的红彩，红彩多已脱落，仅存零星痕迹。墓室正上方偏西有一长方形天井，南北长 2.2、东西宽 1.2 米。

葬具为石棺一具，东西向置于墓室中部，长 2.4、宽 0.71~0.97、高 0.82~1.2 米。

石棺内有 2 具骨架，保存完好，南侧人骨仰身直肢，北侧人骨侧身直肢，略压于南侧人骨左臂之上。南侧骨架外裹有三层布，最里一层为白布。北侧人骨也裹有数层布，口内含有一枚东罗马查士丁尼一世（公元 527~565 年）金币。

石棺有线刻图案，分布在帮板、挡板和盖板上，内容主要有伏羲女娲、星宿、四神和守护神，局部贴金。镌刻线条优美，自然流畅。左侧帮板，

甬道石门
Stone Gate of Vault Passage

墓室砖壁红彩痕迹
Trace of Red Color on Brick
Wall of Tomb Chamber

中间刻一龙，龙身修长，作腾飞状，长尾后扬，周围布满如意云纹。右侧帮板饰一虎，长，张口露齿，双目圆瞪，身有条状斑纹。

前端挡板中部刻一门，门框涂红彩，门上有三排乳钉，乳钉贴金。门楣上方刻尖拱形似龛楣的门额，两侧各有一飞翔的朱雀。门柱两侧各有一守护神相对立于覆莲座上，面均略向内侧，头后有圆形头光，卷发束髻，深目，高鼻，耳轮较大，戴有耳

石棺开启现场
Opening Stone Coffin on Site

石棺内人骨
Two Skeletons inside Stone Coffin

石棺贴金痕迹
Trace of Gild on
Stone Coffin

坠，上唇有外撇八字须，颈部戴宽带形项圈，上身祖露，肩披帔帛，缠绕于双臂，末端下垂至莲座，腰穿短裙，跣足，右一手持戟。门下方正中为一亚腰形火坛，火坛分三层，周壁饰三角纹并贴金。中

间为一层台面，之下悬挂铃形饰物。火坛上烟雾升腾，火坛两侧向上伸出两支莲朵。后端挡板刻玄武，玄武之后立一守护神，头后有圆形头光，以带束发，结成花状，深目，高鼻，阔嘴，上身祖露，肌肉发达，形象威猛，右手握长柄环首刀，举于头上方。

盖板线刻伏羲女娲图。右侧为伏羲，左侧为女娲，均作人首蛇身，蛇尾内卷，未相交，身着敞口交领宽袖衣，身饰鳞片。伏羲戴小冠，双手捧弯月于头上方，女娲盘髻，腕戴镯，双手捧日于头上方。中间有浮云，周围为星宿。

墓志规格较小，志盖盝顶形，素面。志文楷书，11行，满行12字，共计126字，简要记载了墓主生平。墓主姓李，名诞，字陁娑，婆罗门种，赵国平棘人，其先伯阳之后，北魏正光（520～525年）年间自罽宾归阙，北周保定四年（564年）薨于万年里宅，春秋五十九，死后被授为邯州刺史，葬中乡里。志文中仅提及其长子为槃提，余未加记载。

墓主李诞北魏正光年间自罽宾来到中土，罽宾是中国汉至唐代对中亚一个国家或地区的译称，指卡菲里斯坦至喀布尔河中下游之间的河谷平原而言，某些时期可能包括克什米尔西部，西北临滑国和昭武九姓诸国。罽宾国人崇尚佛法，公元1～3世纪间，罽宾成为佛教中心之一，尤其是阿毗昙和小乘学的中心，在佛教的东传过程中起着极其重要的作用，《隋书·西域列传》中载"罽宾国，在葱岭南，去京师万二千二百里。……其俗尤信佛法"，中土向西求法者，宾也是必游之地。太祖宇文泰因其为婆罗门种。屡蒙赏，婆罗门为天竺四大种姓中

金币正面
Front of Gold Coin

金币背面
Back of Gold Coin

石棺右侧帮板线刻虎头
Incised Tiger Head on Right
Side of Coffin

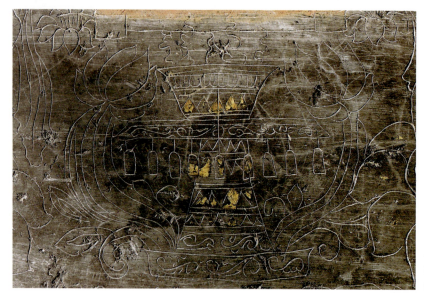

石棺前挡板线刻火坛
Incised Fire Altar on Front
Board of Stone Coffin

最高贵的种姓，专门从事宗教和祭祀活动。墓主为婆罗门种，祖籍天竺应没多大问题。

出土的石棺四侧及盖板均有精美线刻，线刻主要纹饰贴金。线刻内容丰富，以中国传统的伏羲、女娲、四神、星宿等题材为主。除外，线刻中还有一些中外文化相结合的图案和外来文化因素，如龛楣状门额、莲花状柱头与柱础、莲蓬形覆莲座、摩尼宝珠以及前后挡板的守护神，这些内容可能与佛教有关。前端挡板下方正中的三段式火坛，与片治肯特壁画墓和瓦尔赫薩"东厂"粟特壁画墓中的火坛形制比较相似，后两处火坛均与琐罗亚斯德教有关，此种教是流行于古代波斯及中亚地区的宗教，由于罽宾西北临滑国和昭武九姓诸国，南接天竺，因此李诞墓线刻火坛可能受到琐罗亚斯德教（传统上，祆教被比定为波斯琐罗亚斯德教）的影响，但也有可能与其它拜火教如印度教（即新婆罗门教）等有关。

李诞墓是目前国内发现的第一座明确记载为婆罗门种人及罽宾国来华人的墓葬。李诞墓的发掘证明西安北郊一带不仅是北周时期粟特人墓地所在，而且是旅居长安的外来人墓葬集中地，并再一次证明北周时期的长安已是中西文化交流和交融的国际化大都市。

（供稿：程林泉 张小丽 张翔宇 王磊 李书镇）

后挡板线刻拓片
Rubbing of Incised Rear
Board of Stone Coffin

墓志拓片
Rubbing of Tomb Epitaph

The Tomb of Li Dan of the Northern Wei is located at Nankang village in a northern suburb of Xi'an City, Shaanxi Province. In September 2005, the tomb was excavated by the Xi'an Municipal Institute of Archaeology and Heritage Protection. The Tomb of Li Dan is a brick structure with a dome ceiling and a long sloping tomb passage, directed to 180 degrees, and composed of a tomb passage, a vault passage, and a tomb chamber. A stone coffin was placed in the center of the chamber, holding two bodies, one of which held a gold coin of the Byzantine Empire in its mouth. The stone coffin was incised with elegant designs: god Fu Xi, goddess Nu Wa and constellations on the cover, blue dragon on the left side, white tiger on the right side, turtle-and-snake *xuanwu* and a guarding spirit on the rear board, and red phoenix, a gate, a guarding spirit, and a fire altar on the front board.

According to the unearthed tomb epitaph, the occupant of the tomb was Li Dan with a styled name Tuosuo. Li Dan's hometown was Pingji of the Zhao State of the Western Territories. He came to the Central Plains from Kophen of Central Asia during the Zhengguang Reign of the Northern Wei (AD 520 - 525). Because of his Brahmana status, Emperor Taizu Yuwen Tai of the Northern Zhou granted him rewards several times. Li Dan died in his home at Wannianli (*li* as an administrative unit) in the fourth year of the Baoding Reign (564) at the age of 59. After his death, he was granted the position *cishi* (provincial governor) of Hanzhou, and buried at Zhongxiangli. The Tomb of Li Dan is the first tomb which clearly recorded the arrival of a Brahmana to China from Kophen of Central Asia. The excavation of the Tomb of Li Dan demonstrates that the northern suburb of today's Xi'an City is not only the site of Sogdian burials of the Northern Zhou period, but also the site of a cemetery of other foreign visitors that lived in the city of Chang'an. It also confirms once again that the city of Chang'an was an international metropolis during the Northern Zhou period.

陕西潼关税村隋代壁画墓

SUI MURAL TOMB AT SHUICUN IN TONGGUAN, SHAANXI

2005年3~12月，陕西省考古研究所在潼关县西北10公里的高桥乡税村发掘了一座大型隋代壁画墓，揭取保存完好的墓道壁画72平方米，出土各类彩绘陶俑等珍贵文物200余件、线刻石棺1具，取得了重要和丰富的收获。

该墓系长斜坡墓道多天井的单室砖墓，平面呈"甲"字形，坐北朝南。由墓道、7个过洞、6个天井、4个壁龛、砖券甬道和墓室等部分组成，水平总长度63.8米，墓室底距地表深16.6米，方向189°。墓葬南60米开外对称分布一对石望柱柱础，说明早年地面原有石刻和神道。墓道长21、宽2.3米。东、西二壁绘出行仪仗图，布局对称，各有46个人物、1匹鞍马和1架列戟。人物皆为男性，平均身高1.25米，头裹幞头，穿圆领直襟窄袖衫，腰系铐带，足蹬靴或鞋，腰间悬挂仪刀、鞶囊、刀子、布袋、弓袋、箭箙等物品，手中或执弓、或擎旗、或举仪刀，排成队列。人物姿态不一，面部表情丰富，神态非常生动。列戟架位于第一过洞口两侧，每架列戟9杆，共计18杆。墓道北壁绘门楼图，门楼为三开间的庑殿顶楼阁建筑。墓道壁画基本采用线勾手法，填色只有黑、红两色，线条流畅，技法纯熟，显系高手画师的作品。

过洞平均进深2.5、宽1.9米，拱形顶，顶部全部塌陷。过洞两壁仅用红色条框分隔，未绘其他内容。

天井平面呈方形，与墓道等宽或稍宽。天井底部两壁各绘一个执弓站立的人物，保存状况不佳。

壁龛对称开凿于第六、第七过洞两壁，平面呈"吕"字形，进深约3、宽1.2、高1米。龛内放置随葬器物。随葬器物以粉彩陶俑为大宗，种类有镇

墓武士俑、镇墓兽、甲骑具装俑、骑马鼓吹俑、笼冠立俑、风帽立俑、小冠立俑、幞头立俑、各种动物俑等。陶俑形体较大，彩绘艳丽，描金涂银，制作精细。

甬道砖券拱形顶，进深6.58、宽1.5、高1.83米。壁画墙皮大面积脱落，可见顶部绘平棋，无纹饰，两壁绘影作木构。甬道内建石门一座、置墓志一合，但均已被盗。

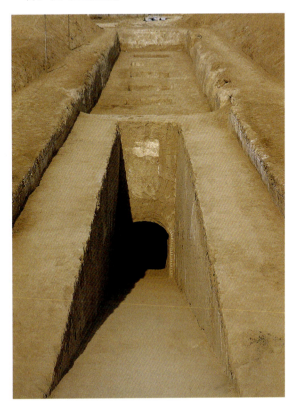

墓葬外景
Outside View of Mural Tomb

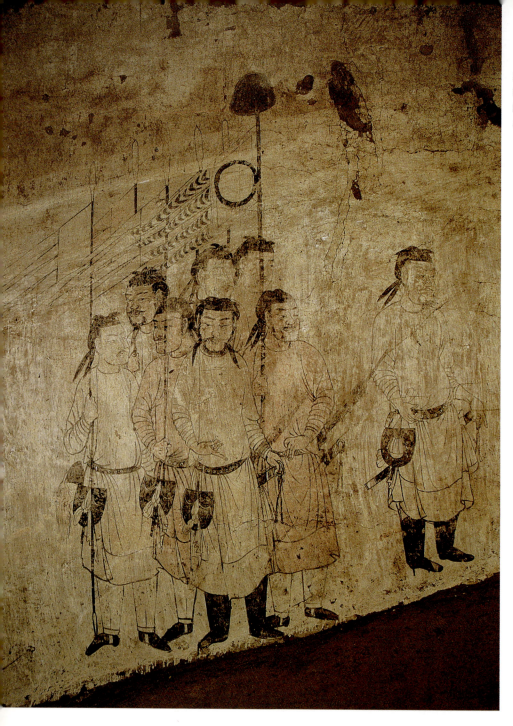

　　墓室平面呈圆形，直径5.9米左右，双层砖券穹隆顶，外层和内层顶距墓室地面分别为8.2米和6.5米。内层顶用烟火熏成黑色，绘星汉图。墓室四壁壁画已完全脱落，从残存的白灰墙皮看，绘有女性人物。

　　墓室内中部偏北置石棺一具，东西向，头部朝西。墓室和石棺内的随葬品经古今数次盗掘已被洗劫一空。石棺全长2.9、宽1.5、高1.5米，由盖板、南北壁板、东西挡板和底板组成，外侧面满布浅减地线刻画，内容有朱雀、玄武、云中仙人车驾、瑞兽等，体量巨大，线刻内容繁复，制作精美。

　　盖板顶面以联珠纹带作框、莲花为节，分隔为龟背甲结构的六边形连续图案。其中完整的六边形单元60个，四周各分布6个三角形和梯形单元。每个单元内各有一个主题图案，地衬流云纹。西边和东边的12个三角形单元中各有一个忍冬花结。其余72个六角形单元和梯形单元中的图案的方向皆指向西，图案的内容基本上以纵轴为中心对称，例

墓道东壁壁画局部
Partial View of Mural on East Wall of Tomb Passage

墓道东壁壁画局部
Partial View of Mural on East Wall of Tomb Passage

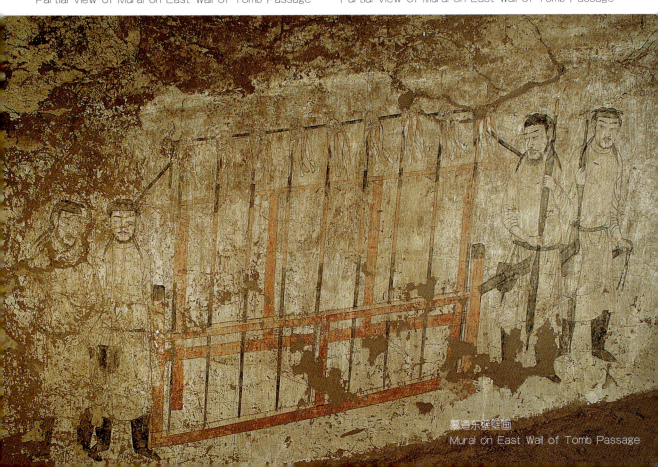

墓道东壁壁画
Mural on East Wall of Tomb Passage

墓道北壁壁画门楼图
Mural of "Gatehouse" on North Wall
of Tomb Passage

如第3格和第5格的主题图案都是"龙",第48格和第51格的主题图案都是"摩尼珠"。每个六边形内的内容皆不相同,已辨认出的有虎、马、牛、羊、鸿雁等动物和摩羯鱼、龙、凤、双头鸟、人首鸟身的各种瑞兽。

西挡板正中刻一座门。门楣刻缠枝忍冬纹、瑞兽,门额刻缠枝宝相花纹、摩尼宝珠,门框刻缠枝忍冬纹。门外正中立一双翅开张、口衔宝珠的朱雀。门两侧各站一戎服门吏,皆面向门的方向,形象动作基本相同。头戴平巾帻,着裲裆、袴褶,腰系鞶带,手拄仪刀。其他还有龙、狮子、花朵、摩尼宝珠等纹饰。

东挡板线刻画的主题内容为玄武和力士。玄武系一蛇缠一龟。龟蛇交缠,头部对望呼应。力士头似狮头,秃顶大耳,脑后生鬣。浑身肌肉隆起,强健有力。佩戴项圈、臂钏、手镯,右手平举,横握一柄环首长刀,刀刃向上,刀身置于脑后。

北壁板线刻画的主题内容为仙人车驾、扈从及鼓吹。有4只虎系驾的辂车1乘,乘车贵妇1人,扈从仙女12名,吹角力士(风伯)3名,击鼓力士(雷公)3名,负鼓力士2名,擎山力士2名,奔走力士1名,飞翔的鹤、凤、摩羯鱼、蜥蜴各1只,其他半身或仅露头部的龙、凤、獬豸、力士、怪兽若干。

墓室顶部壁画星汉图
Mural of "Constellations" on Top of Tomb Chamber

石棺浅刻画局部
Partial View of Incised Image on Stone Coffin

扈从人物皆为女性，形象装束基本相同，头梳高髻，上身着窄袖襦衫，外套半袖，袖口轩敞并有皱褶，下穿长裙，束腰上提至胸部。画面的布局为：中部亦即整个画面的中心为一驾车，车的两侧及前、后方为执不同物品的扈从仙女、禽兽和鼓吹。

南壁板线刻画的主题内容与北壁板相仿，布局基本对称，不同的是仙人皆为男性，驾车的是龙。

底板四侧以联珠纹分框，刻奔跑的鸟兽。

根据墓葬形制和随葬品与石棺线刻画的风格判断，该墓系隋代墓葬。根据壁画列戟图的列戟杆数分析，墓主人应系杨隋皇室成员，最低身份为亲王，不排除生前做过太子或身后追赠太子的可能。

潼关税村隋代壁画墓是我国隋唐考古史和美术考古史上的重大发现，是迄今为止发掘的规模最大、等级最高的隋代墓葬，为探索杨隋皇族墓地和隋代高等级墓葬制度提供了线索。

（供稿：李明 刘呆运）

石棺浅刻画局部
Partial View of Incised Image on Stone Coffin

From March to December 2005, the Shaanxi Provincial Institute of Archaeology excavated a large mural tomb of the Sui dynasty at Shuicun village in Gaoqiao, which lies 10 km northwest of the town of Tongguan County, Shaanxi Province. This Sui tomb is 63.8 m in total length and orientated so that it faces the south. The layout of the tomb is in a shape of the character "甲", composed of a square brick tomb chamber and a series of extended structural units, including a long sloping tomb passage, seven passing tunnels, six corridor shafts, four niches, and a vaulted passage with a brick arched top.

The sloping tomb passage is 21 m long and 2.3 m wide, with fairly well-preserved murals on the east, west, and north walls. The murals on the east and west walls are scenes of procession and guards of honor, and the scenes on the two murals are basically symmetrical. On each mural, there are 46 human figures, one saddled horse, and a *ji*-halberd stand. The human figures are all males with different facial expressions, holding either a bow, a flag, or a ceremonial knife. The two *ji*-halberd stands are painted at the opening of the first passing tunnel, one on each side of the tunnel and each holding nine ji-halberds. The north wall of the tomb passage is painted with a gatehouse, which is a storied pavilion with three rooms and a hip roof. The seven passing tunnels are all earth structures with arched tops. On both sides of the sixth and seventh tunnels, four niches are cut in the walls, storing pottery figurines and pottery funerary object models. Inside the vaulted passage, a stone gate was built to hold the epitaph.

The layout of the tomb chamber is round with a diameter of approximately 5.9 m. The arched roof of the chamber was built with two layers of bricks. The inner layer is 5.6 m high and the outer layer is 8.2 m high. The top of the inner layer roof is painted with star images, with the sky represented by a black background, and the Milky Way and other constellations by white lines and dots. Unfortunately, the paintings on the four walls of the chamber had all peeled away. A stone coffin was placed slightly north of the center of the chamber and orientated in the east-west direction. The stone coffin is 2.9 m long, 1.38 m wide, and 1.41 m high, and it is incised on the outside with complicated contents in a graceful style.

Unearthed funerary objects are mainly pottery figurines painted with color, including the types of guarding warrior, guarding animal, armored rider, mounted musician, standing figure, animal figure, etc. These pottery figurines are vividly colored, delicately made, and painted with gold and silver powders.

Based on the structure and layout of the tomb as well as the style of the funerary objects and stone coffin carvings, the tomb at Shuicun village is dated to the Sui dynasty. Further, based on the number of the *ji*-halberds painted in the passage, the occupant of this tomb should be a member of the Sui royal family, at least with a status of prince. The possibility can not be excluded that the occupant of the tomb was even a crown prince during his life or was granted this title after his death.

陶步卒俑
Pottery Infant Figurine

陶骑马俑
Pottery Mounted Figurine

陕西西安
唐大明宫丹凤门遗址

DANFENG GATE SITE OF TANG DAMING PALACE IN XI'AN, SHAANXI

丹凤门遗址位于陕西省西安市北郊二马路南。2005 年 9 月～2006 年 1 月，为配合唐大明宫遗址的规划保护工程，中国社会科学院考古研究所西安唐城队对该遗址进行了大规模的考古发掘，发掘面积 8000 余平方米。

丹凤门遗址是唐大明宫遗址的正南门，建造在大明宫南城墙中部（也即唐长安城外郭城的北城墙东段），是高宗以后的唐朝皇帝出入宫城的主要通道。门址向北正对大明宫正殿含元殿，门外向南为宽 170 余米的丹凤门大街。门上建有高大的门楼，是皇帝宣布大赦和改元的重要场所，故规格在大明宫诸门中为最高。始建年代可能是唐高宗龙朔二年（662 年），唐末废毁。

从发掘情况得知，丹凤门是被火烧后废弃的，各门道的路面与两壁大部分火烧痕迹明显。门址上部的建筑已破坏无存，现仅存有部分夯土结构的门墩台底部，其中门址中门道以东大部分已被破坏至当时（唐代）地面以下，门址中门道以西至西墩台保存相对较好，尚高出当时地面近 2 米。虽然如此，但门的形制还很清楚。

丹凤门共有五个门道，平面呈长方形。门址墩台东西长 74.5、南北宽（进深）30 余米，方向北偏东 1°20′。城门的包砖和墙皮多已被破坏，仅门址西墩台南侧与城墙衔接的转角处和由东向西的第四门道两侧以及第五门道东南隔墙底部尚残留少许。从包砖遗痕来看，城门外侧的包砖壁厚约 1 米许。在砖壁外，尚有部分散水的铺砖遗痕，散水宽度不详。门道两侧排叉柱间的包砖厚约 0.4～0.5 米。

五个门道的建筑形式相同，均是两壁立排叉柱的木构架"过梁式"城门。五个门道除第一门道全部、第二门道南部被后期路沟及其他设施破坏外，其余各门道保存相对较好且形制基本上清楚。门道东西宽约 9、南北进深 31 米（不含包砖壁，其中第二门道至第五门道间的夯土隔墙南北现存 24 米）。各门道之间的夯土隔墙厚 2.9 米。门道两侧都有排叉柱的柱础坑，柱础石多已破坏无存。其中在中门道东侧门槛以北第一础坑位、第四门道东侧门槛以北第一础坑位、第四门道西侧门槛以南第一础坑位、第五门道西侧门槛以南第一础坑位尚存留有长方形础石。础石为青石质，长 0.7～0.75、宽 0.59～0.63、厚 0.32 米。在础石

丹凤门遗址俯视（上南下北）
Top View of Danfeng Gate Site (south at top of photograph)

中央还凿有长15、宽11、深5厘米的长方形榫眼。柱础坑一般都是长方形的，长约0.8、宽约0.7米，深度不等。各柱础坑相距多在0.5米左右，础坑的底部都铺一层粗砂，当是为稳固柱础所垫的。

门道的中部略偏南均设有门槛。从保存相对较好的中门道和第五门道的门槛结构来看，门槛两端为青石制成，中间部分为木质门槛。木质门槛均已烧毁，唯留有长约2.7、宽约24、深约0.2米左右的沟槽，沟槽内尚残留有少许木质烧灼遗痕。木质门槛两端的青石多已无存，唯在中门道的第五门道门槛东端残存少许，其中中门道东端的青石残存较多，青石截面呈长方形，表面光平，无纹饰。东西残长1.4、残高0.8、厚0.39米左右。

门槛两端的门砧石，都已破坏无存。唯留有基

丹凤门遗址平、剖面示意图
Plan and Section Profile
of Danfeng Gate Site

北

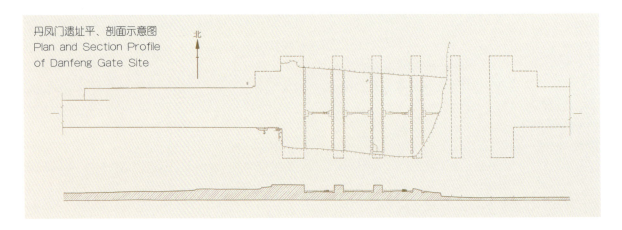

西墩台外侧砌砖残迹
Remaining Bricks on Outer Side
of Western Base Platform

西墩台东侧（由北向南）
Eastern Side of West-
ern Base Platform
(from north to south)

西墩台与西侧门道（由南向北）
Western Base Platform and
Gate Passage on Western Side
(from south to north)

第四门道东侧隔墙（由北向南）
Division Wall on Eastern Side
of Fourth Gate Passage

中门道门限（槛）（由东向西）
Gate Threshold on Central
Gate Passage

础坑位。础坑平面为长方形，南北长1.8、东西0.68、深0.35米。

每个门道路面亦被火烧过，其表面非常坚硬。另外，门道路面在门槛处较高，由门槛向北、南（门内、外侧）渐低，呈坡形。路面上未发现有车辙痕迹，也未发现有铺砖或铺石痕迹，但路面上的夯窝痕迹明显。以此推测，当时门道路面上可能铺有木板或其他设施。

关于上城楼的"马道"（即慢道），应在城门内侧两端靠城墙处。我们于城门内侧东、西两侧各发掘了一段城垣，发掘表明：在西城门墩的西侧有一东西长8、南北宽5米的"平台"，由此平台再向西去长54米处，则向内（南）矩折3.5米，然后西去为宽9米的城墙，这一矩折部分，当是上城的马道。另外，在马道的北侧以及东端矩折部分还留有砌砖残迹。城门东边的墩台、城墙和马道虽已破坏，但从发掘出的基础部分来看，与城门西边的发掘一致，是东西相对称的，东边亦当有同样的上城马道。

考古发掘出土的遗物相对较少，主要见有砖、瓦、瓦当、鸱尾、门钉、瓷器、唐三彩残片等。其中以砖、瓦最多。砖多为素面长方形砖，瓦为板瓦和筒瓦，有素面、青揭和绿釉三种，而且瓦的体形比一般的唐代瓦大而厚重。另外，还发掘出土了带有铭文的砖、瓦1件，长砖表面模印有"西坊天宝□年六□"铭文，1件板瓦残块边沿模印有"天宝四月官瓦"铭文。

通过这次考古发掘，最终澄清了有关丹凤门是五个门道（文献记载）还是三个门道（钻探结果）的学术难题。揭露出来的丹凤门遗址规模之大、门道之宽、马道之长，均为目前隋唐考古乃至中国古代城址考古所发现的城门之最，充分体现出唐朝建筑的恢弘气派。丹凤门遗址的考古发掘为唐长安城的考古、中国古代都城考古以及中国古代建筑史的研究提供了第一手的科学资料。

（供稿：何岁利）

"官"字款白瓷碗底
Base of White Porcelain Bowl with
"*guan*" (official) mark

三彩器残件
Broken Three-color-glaze Ware

残留的础石与砌砖
Remaining Base-rock and Bricks

丹凤门西侧"马道"（由西向东）
"Horse-way" on the Western Side of
Danfeng Gate (from west to east)

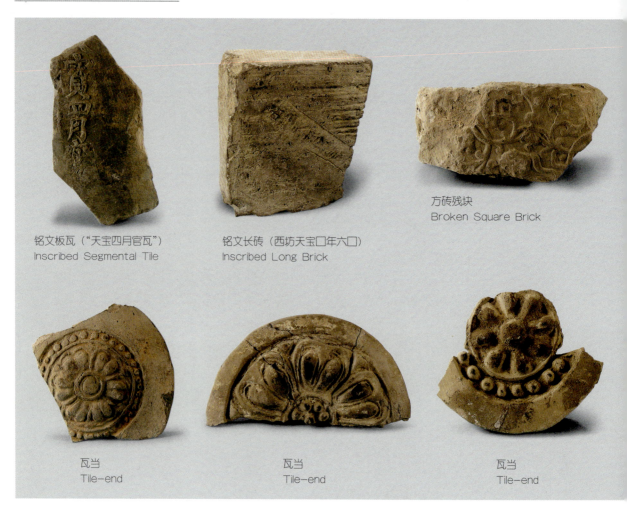

铭文板瓦（"天宝四月官瓦"）
Inscribed Segmental Tile

铭文长砖（西坊天宝□年六□）
Inscribed Long Brick

方砖残块
Broken Square Brick

瓦当
Tile-end

瓦当
Tile-end

瓦当
Tile-end

The Danfeng (Red Phoenix) Gate is the front south gate of the Daming (Grandly Bright) Palace compound of the Tang dynasty, which is directed strictly northward to the Hanyuandian, the central palace hall of the Daming Palace compound. After Emperor Gaozong (AD 659 - 683), the Danfeng Gate was the major passageway for emperors to pass in and out of the Daming Palace compound.

Starting from September 2005, the Xi'an Tang City Archaeological Team of the Institute of Archaeology of the Chinese Academy of Social Sciences has launched large scale excavations on the Danfeng Gate site. It has been revealed through the excavations that the base platform of the gate foundation is 74 m long in the east-west direction, and over 30 m wide in the north-south direction (depth of the gate). There are five gate passages and each of them measures 9 m wide. The post-base holes along the two sides of the passages are densely distributed. On every passage, a gate threshold is set up slightly south of the passage center. Inside the Danfeng Gate, two "horse-ways" (*madao*), both measuring 54 m long, are symmetrically allocated along the wall, starting right from the eastern and western ends of the Gate. The artifacts unearthed from the Danfeng Gate site are mainly bricks and tiles.

Of all the city gate sites discovered from the Sui-Tang archaeology and even the entire Chinese archaeology of ancient cities, the Danfeng Gate site is the most massive with regard to the scale of the site, the width of its passages, and the length of its horse-ways. The excavation of the Danfeng Gate site therefore provides first-hand scientific data for the study of the archaeology of the Tang city of Chang'an, the archaeology of ancient Chinese capital cities, and the history of ancient Chinese architecture.

河南洛阳
唐安国相王孺人墓

TANG TOMBS OF TWO WIVES OF KING XIANG OF AN STATE IN LUOYANG, HENAN

2005年3～6月，洛阳市第二文物工作队为配合洛阳市新区道路建设在隋唐洛阳城遗址西南角的龙门原上发掘唐墓2座，两墓呈东西分布，相距约150米。据出土墓志，两墓分别为唐安国相王（唐睿宗李旦公元705～710年封号）孺人唐氏（M49）、崔氏墓（M50）。

两墓形制基本相同，为明券单室穹隆顶砖室墓，由墓道、过洞、天井、壁龛、甬道、墓室组成。方向均为183°。M49长35.1米，有4过洞、3天井、4壁龛。M50长32.12米，有5过洞、5天井、4壁龛。

两墓墓道、过洞、天井两侧均保存了部分壁画，甬道及墓室内仅见大量绘有壁画的剥落的白灰残片。根据壁画残迹可知，其做法是先在土壁或砖壁上涂一层厚约2～3毫米草拌泥，再刷一层厚1～2毫米的白灰，然后在磨光的灰面粉底上作画。

在两墓墓道和过洞两壁均保存了大面积壁画，共约70平方米。壁画内容大体一致，均为"出行图"。墓道东西两侧左青龙、右白虎，其后为人牵马及骆驼图。唐氏墓共存壁画人物38个，马4，骆驼2，青龙、白虎各1。人物有门吏、武士、伎乐、仆人、侏儒等。

墓道东壁所绘青龙长5.4米，龙头，额以上残缺，双目圆睁，颔下有须，昂首吐舌，龙鳞用墨线勾画，加以青蓝色，四足腾空，身下祥云弥漫，飞鸟翱翔。

牵马驼图为二人牵马一人牵骆驼。牵骆驼者为胡人，身材矮小，头戴笼帽，络腮胡，浓眉高鼻朱唇，身穿翻领长袍，腰束带，脚穿黑鞋，左手蜷缩身侧，右手置于胸部。身后骆驼头部漫漶漶不清，橙黄色毛发，双峰，带鞍行走状。

墓道西壁门吏头裹幞头，圆睁双眼，朱唇，蓄胡须，长髯，身穿橙色团领长袍，腰束带，深灰色长筒靴，腰佩剑，右手贴胸前，左手握剑身，上身

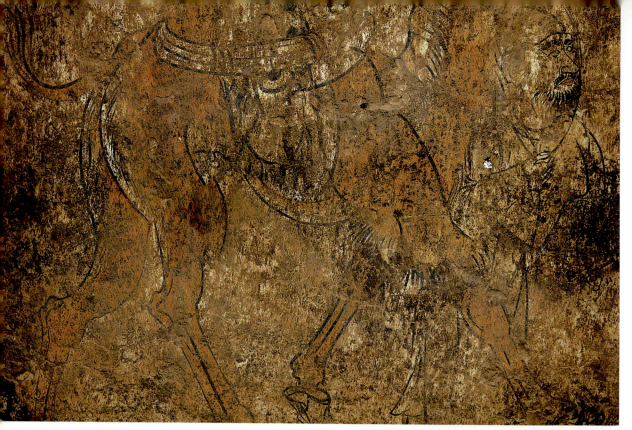

唐氏墓墓道东壁壁画胡人牵驼
Foreigner Leading Camel in Mural on Eastern Wall
of Sloping Passage in Lady Tang's Tomb

前倾，若恭身迎人之状。画幅高1.5米。

　　墓道北壁影作木结构阁楼，底部脱落。阁楼为歇山顶，垂脊，直棂窗，出檐涂红色，出檐下垂雕花木板，转角木柱及窗棂均涂朱红，木栏杆下有卧棂，栏杆与出檐间用涂黑木柱承接。

　　过洞东壁所绘侏儒，头裹幞头，五官清晰，身穿团领束腰长袍，两手笼袖拱于胸前，高66厘米。西壁壁画人物与东壁相对应。

　　崔氏墓存壁画人物14个，马、驼各2，青龙、白虎各1。墓道东西两壁壁画内容基本相同，剥落比较严重。

　　过洞、天井东西两壁尚存6个人物，大多头部及上半身脱落。东壁过洞二下部的武士，头上部脱落，瞪眼高鼻，张口吐舌，络腮胡，耸肩缩颈，面目狰狞，身穿橘黄短袄，束腰，紧身裤，深灰长筒靴，左手裸袖抓剑身，右手作拔剑之势，画幅高1.2米。

　　两墓均遭多次盗掘，但仍出土了红陶鼓吹伎乐骑马俑、人物俑和马、骆驼、狗、羊、鸡、猪等动物模型以及石翁仲、瓷器等。

　　唐氏、崔氏史书均无记载。据墓志知她们均为大唐安国相王孺人。安国相王是唐睿宗在公元

唐氏墓墓道西壁壁画门吏
Door Attendant in Mural on Western Wall
of Sloping Passage in Lady Tang's Tomb

唐氏墓过洞东壁壁画侏儒
Dwarf in Mural on Eastern Wall of
Passing Tunnel in Lady Tang's Tomb

唐氏墓墓道西壁壁画武士
Warrior in Mural on Western Wall of
Sloping Passage in Lady Tang's Tomb

唐氏墓过洞东壁壁画武士
Warrior in Mural on Eastern Wall of
Passing Tunnel in Lady Tang's Tomb

崔氏墓墓道西壁壁画门吏
Door Attendant in Mural on Western Wall of
Sloping Passage in Lady Cui's Tomb

唐氏墓出土骑马伎乐俑
Horse-riding Entertainer Figurines from Lady Tang's Tomb

唐氏墓出土骑马伎乐俑
Horse-riding Entertainer Figurines from Lady Tang's Tomb

唐氏墓出土风帽俑
Cloaked Figurine from
Lady Tang's Tomb

705～710 年的封号。关于唐氏，墓志记载比较明确，其祖父唐剑，《两唐书》有传。崔氏墓志无存，其生平不详，但据墓志盖"□唐安国相王故孺人清河崔氏墓志铭"，也可知她埋葬的大体年代。

　　两墓壁画均为单栏，壁画内容相似，但绘画风格迥异。唐氏墓笔法细腻，刻画人物传神；崔氏墓

用笔粗豪，雄浑苍劲。虽然由于壁画脱落严重，已难窥全貌，但仍从中领略到唐代绘画的独特魅力。

　　两墓墓葬，纪年明确，时代特征明显，是研究武周及中宗时期的埋葬制度、壁画艺术、社会风尚等方面重要的实物资料。

（供稿：史家珍 吴业恒）

The two tombs of the Tang dynasty are located at Longmenyuan in the southwestern corner of the site of the Sui-Tang Luoyang City. The excavation of the two tombs from March to June 2005 was carried out by the Second Archaeological Team of Luoyang City as a rescue program for the road construction project in the New District of today's Luoyang City, Henan Province. According to the unearthed tomb epitaphs, the two tombs belonged to Lady Tang and Lady Cui, respectively. Both ladies were *ruren* (wife) of Anguo Xiangwang (King Xiang of An State), the title that was granted to Emperor Ruizong Li Dan of the Tang dynasty during the years from AD 705 to 710 before his enthronement.

The two tombs are both single-chamber brick structures, orientated in the north-south direction, and composed of a long sloping passage, passing tunnel, shaft, niche, vaulted passage and chamber. The total length of the

tombs is over 30 m. Both tombs were buried with a large amount of lively terracotta figurines as well as stone *wengzhong* human statues and porcelain wares. In both tombs, murals of about 70 sq m were preserved on both sides of the sloping passage and passing tunnel. The contents of the murals in both tombs are generally similar, all depicting scenes of procession. From the perspective of painting style, however, each tomb is distinctive in its own way. The murals in Lady Tang's tomb were lively depicted with delicate strokes, whereas the murals in Lady Cui's tomb were boldly depicted with powerful strokes.

The murals in the two tombs contain multiple human figures and rich contents. The murals in the two tombs, therefore, provide invaluable sources for the study of mural art of the Tang dynasty, and for the study of the mortuary practice, dress and ornament style, and social customs of the middle Tang period.

江苏扬州
唐宋城东门遗址的发掘

EXCAVATION AT THE SITE OF EASTERN GATE OF THE TANG-SONG YANGZHOU CITY IN YANGZHOU, JIANGSU

扬　州唐宋城东门遗址位于江苏省扬州市城区东关街和泰州路的交汇处，东关街横贯遗址，发现于2000年初。2004年8～11月、2005年5～9月，由中国社会科学院考古研究所、南京博物院、扬州市文物考古组组成的江苏扬州唐城考古队继续对其进行了发掘清理，在主城墙和主城门处揭露出了唐、五代、北宋、南宋时期的城墙包砖、主城门、露道等，在主城门以东清理出了形成于南宋初期的瓮城、便门、露道、城壕等遗迹现象，在南宋瓮城东墙之下还解剖发现了北宋的出城露道。出土遗物主要有唐宋时期铭文城砖、唐至清的瓷片和铜钱等。

清理出的唐代主城墙被叠压在五代和两宋时期的门址之下，用黏土夹杂砂土夯筑而成，夯层厚10～12厘米。城墙外侧有厚约0.9米的南北向包砖，砖一般长35、宽17.5、厚6.5厘米。砌法有两种，一种是面砖为一排顺砖，内填两排丁砖，与面砖错缝；另一种是面砖为一排丁砖，内填一排丁砖和一排顺砖。两种砌法隔层错缝使用，砌砖之间用黄黏土粘合。

五代时期的城墙较之唐代向东移了约2米，城墙用黄灰色杂土夯就，夯层厚5～10厘米。城墙包砖被叠压在宋代城墙包砖之下，采用平砖错缝顺砌的方式，所用砌砖一般长43、宽23、厚6厘米。在

城墙包砖东侧的南宋瓮城内地面之下约0.8米深处，解剖发现有五代时期的城墙外铺砖面。

北宋城墙外侧包砖在五代城墙外包砖的基础上

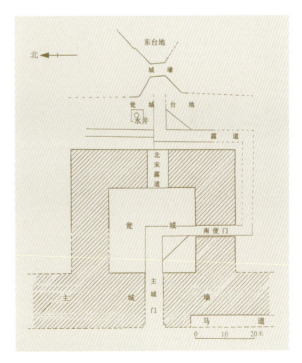

唐宋城东门遗址总平面示意图
Grand Site Plan of the Eastern Gate
of the Tang-Song Period

145

东门主门道（由西向东）
Front Gate Passageway
(from west to east)

主城门南部唐~南宋时期包砖
（由北向南）
Out Layer Wall Bricks Dated to
the Tang–Southern Song
Periods from the Southern
Section of the Front Gate

向内收缩了约1.2米。城墙夯土为黄黏土，夯层厚约10厘米。主城墙的包砖采用一顺一丁和半砖丁砌的方法，所用砌砖多残断，只有少量的整砖，一般长37、宽18.5、厚5.2厘米，填砖长34.5、宽17.7、厚5厘米。

北宋时期的主门道仅揭露出东部，东西6.45米，外口宽5.07、门砧石内宽6.07米。门道两侧为砖砌边壁，砌砖叠压在五代时期的砌砖之上。砌砖采用二顺一丁和全为丁砖两种砌法。主门道内的两块方形门砧石南北对应，高出外侧露道约7厘米，石上有边长28厘米的方孔。

在南宋时期瓮城东墙夯土之下，解剖发现有保存较好的北宋时期露道。该段露道呈东西向，南北宽约5.8米，路面砖和路心石破损较为严重，有多条车辙印痕残存。露道铺砖所用楔形砖，两端面经过加工，铺砌时大面朝上，用砖长边29、短边25.5、高10、厚约6厘米。该段路面铺砖之下，垫有厚约7厘米的黄黏土层，与主门道内北宋露道的做法相同。

南宋时期对东门进行了改建和扩建，除了加厚主城墙包砖将主门道内缩变窄之外，还在主城门外加筑瓮城并疏浚加固城壕，并在东台地上增设军事防御设施，形成了一个以瓮城为中心，由东台地、城壕、瓮城台地、瓮城和主城墙构成的多重防御体

五代城墙外侧铺砖（上东下西）
Outside-wall Floor Bricks Dated to the Five
Dynasties (from west to east)

北宋时期露道（由东向西）
Opening Passageway Covered with Stone and Bricks,
Dated to the Northern Song (from east to west)

系。南宋时期的东门是一个结构复杂、功能齐全、水陆并重、设施完备的城防工事。

南宋时期主城墙在北宋城墙的基础上向东加宽了约0.8米。包砖采用"露齿龈"做法，每层收分约2厘米，底层砌砖为立砖横铺，以上均采用二顺一丁，错缝平铺，底层立砖与平砖之间的收分约为5厘米。

南宋主城门门道也在北宋城门的基础上向内收缩，形成了宽约4.1米的南宋时期主城门。北宋门砧石以西的门道部分，南宋在北宋的基础上两侧边壁各向内收约0.95米，使得门道内收与城门外口等宽。揭露出来的南宋主城门东部东西约7.2米，门道两侧边壁为砖砌直立壁面，与城墙外侧包砖不同。

南宋瓮城紧邻主城门东侧，瓮城的北、东、南三面城墙厚度分别为12.04、12.2、12.9米，其中南墙上辟有一便门。瓮城内平面形状略呈梯形，东西进深28.3米，东部南北面阔31.5米，西部南北面阔33.75米。瓮城城墙均由夯土夯筑而成，仅基础部分保存较好。城墙内外两面包砖虽大多无存，但基槽清晰。面砖采用"露齿龈"做法，大约每层内收约1厘米。

瓮城内地面铺砖为平砖错缝顺铺，铺砌规整，铺砖面平整。瓮城内地面东北部最高，东北角与排水沟的最大高差达0.6米，当是为了便于瓮城内积水经由南便门边的排水沟流出城外。

瓮城外以东为一东西23、南北60米左右、高出东侧城壕约5.4米的台地。台地上有出城露道、便道等。

瓮城台地东侧的城壕，只发掘清理了瓮城中轴线附近的部分。清理出来的城壕部分，平面呈亚腰形，在和主城门东西大致对应的部位，城壕收缩至最窄，形成南北长5.3、东西宽约4米的狭窄空间。城壕中堆积大量淤泥，故推测原为水壕。在瓮城台地和城壕东侧的东台地的外边，都设有防止水流冲刷的砌砖护岸。从发掘情况推测，城壕南北两端应与东侧的运河连通，城壕内的水应该是从北向南流动，城壕和大运河环绕着东台地。城壕之上，应该设有壕桥之类设施以连通瓮城台地与东台地。

东台地是位于瓮城东侧的一个高于城壕的台地，台地顶面的高度与西侧的瓮城外地面高度基本相当。揭露出的东台地部分东西约30、南北约15米。从发掘的情况并结合文献资料推测东台地西、南、北三面为城壕，东临大运河，台地被城壕和运河环绕而成为水中环岛。

根据发掘结果并结合文献来看，瓮城在元代末

南宋瓮城东墙外露道细部
Details of Opening Passageway Outside
the Eastern Wall of the Southern Song Barbican

铭文砖
Inscribed Bricks, From Tang
to Qing Dynasties

石球
Stone Balls

年被彻底毁弃，即元代基本沿用了南宋时期瓮城，但封闭了城壕两端的水口并在城壕内修建有小型建筑。

东门遗址发掘出土了大量的唐至明清时期的瓷器、铜钱、铜器、铁器、铭文砖等遗物。所出瓷片涵盖了唐至明清各主要窑口，特别是在瓮城外侧解剖到的唐代灰坑中还发现了唐代青花瓷残片，扩大了唐青花在扬州的发现范围。所出铭文城砖的时代有唐、五代、两宋和明清，内容多为烧造地和烧造者的归属和身份。

扬州是一座有着近2500年历史的古城，而东门遗址沿用的1200多年，基本涵盖了扬州城市发展的后半段。东门遗址的变迁，既反映了唐代"春风十里，夜市千灯"，宋代"淮左明都，竹西佳处"以及明清"繁华今胜昔"的繁华和兴盛，也反映了五代时期"人烟灭绝，赤地百里。残垣断壁，满目疮痍"，两宋之际"废池乔木，犹厌言兵"以及"扬州十日"的沧桑和兴替。

唐宋城东门遗址的发现，对于研究扬州城的历史沿革具有重要的意义。目前揭露出的遗迹现象表明，东门是扬州宋大城四座城门中结构最复杂、保存最完整的一座，这对于研究扬州城市建设和城市布局演变有着重要的意义，也印证了《嘉靖维扬志·宋大城图》中关于东门的有关记载。

（供稿：汪勃 刘涛 匡朝晖）

南宋瓮城东墙外铺砖地面、露道、便道、漫道（由东向西）
Brick-covered Floor, Opening Passageway, Side Passage and Sideway Outside the Eastern Wall of the Southern Song Barbican (from east to west)

南宋城壕西侧护岸局部（由东向西）
Part of the Brick Embankment on the Western Bank of the City Moat Dated to the Southern Song (from east to west)

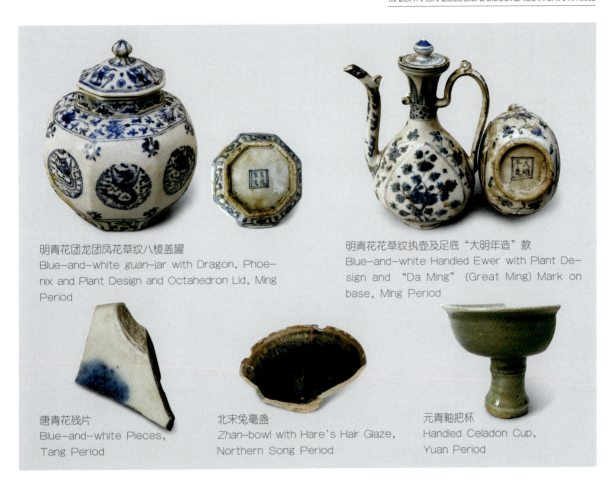

明青花团龙团凤花草纹八棱盖罐
Blue–and–white *guan*–jar with Dragon, Phoe-
nix and Plant Design and Octahedron Lid, Ming
Period

明青花花草纹执壶及足底 "大明年造" 款
Blue–and–white Handled Ewer with Plant Design and "Da Ming" (Great Ming) Mark on
base, Ming Period

唐青花残片
Blue–and–white Pieces,
Tang Period

北宋兔毫盏
Zhan–bowl with Hare's Hair Glaze,
Northern Song Period

元青釉把杯
Handled Celadon Cup,
Yuan Period

The Eastern Gate site of Yangzhou City of the Tang-Song period is located at Dongguanjie (Eastern Gate Street) to the west of the ancient Grand Canal in today's Yangzhou City, Jiangsu Province. The site was first discovered in early 2000 and then excavated in two field seasons from August to November 2004 and from May to September 2005. Jointly organized by the Institute of Archaeology of the Chinese Academy of Social Sciences, the Museum of Nanjing, and the Yangzhou Municipal Bureau of Cultural Relics, archaeologists at the site exposed an area of nearly 2,000 sq m and unearthed a series of defense features, including the main city wall, the front gate passageway, the open passageway, and the barbican structure dated to the Southern Song dynasty. Also unearthed through excavations were a large amount of inscribed wall bricks dating to the Tang and Song dynasties, bronze coinages and porcelain pieces ranging in date from the Tang to the Qing dynasties. The basic appearance of the Eastern Gate site has thus been revealed. At the location of the main city wall and the front city gate, out layer wall bricks dated to the succeeding periods of the Tang, Five Dynasties, Northern Song, and Southern Song were discovered, as were features such as the front gate and the opening passageway. To the east of the front gate, various features were identified, including the barbican structure first built in the early Southern Song, the side gate, the opening passageway, and the city moat. Underneath the eastern wall of the Southern Song barbican, the exit passage of the Northern Song period was discovered. The results of the excavations indicate that the Eastern Gate was initially built in the Tang period. It was afterwards utilized and repaired during the Five Dynasties and the Northern Song, repaired and expanded during the Southern Song, and eventually abandoned at the end of the Yuan dynasty. During the Southern Song period, the Eastern Gate was a complex, fully functioning, amphibious, and well facilitated defense system, which was composed of the main city wall, the front gate, the barbican, the side gate, the moat and the embankment. The discovery of the Eastern Gate of the Tang - Song period is therefore highly significant for the study of the historical development of Yangzhou City.

天津蓟县
千像寺石刻造像群

BUDDHIST FIGURE CARVINGS
AT QIANXIANGSI IN JIXIAN, TIANJIN

千像寺造像群位于天津市蓟县官庄镇联合村北，盘山东麓白水峪之南，东南距蓟县县城12.5公里，西距盘山风景区3公里。

早在20世纪70～80年代，天津市文物管理处考古队、蓟县文物保管所已注意到"千像寺遗址前后巨石上有许多线刻佛像"。1982年，天津市人民政府将千像寺石刻列入天津市文物保护单位。为了加强千像寺造像群的保护，天津市文化遗产保护中心自2003年至2005年对千像寺造像群进行"拉网式"调查和多次复查，并采集造像本体信息。目前，造像群已申报第六批全国重点文物保护单位。

根据调查，千像寺造像集中分布于千像寺遗址的西北、东北、西南和东南部的孤石或崖壁上，处于盘山侵蚀丘陵区的浅山与平原交接地带，核部为花岗岩体，地势北高南低，岩石风化显著。根据已测绘的《天津蓟县千像寺造像平面图》，造像的空间分布实测正投影面积为0.4平方公里，海拔高程介于100～200米，最高处造像与最低处造像的高差为95米。

迄今已在124处地点发现535尊线刻造像。造像全部采用阴线刻的技法，除少数造像略显繁复，大部分造像造型简练，线条粗放。造像的高度不等，立姿高度一般为1.1～1.5米，最大者2.2米，坐姿高度一般为0.9米，最小者0.6米。刊刻的花岗岩质石块表面不加任何修整，依岩石的形状布

盘山祐唐千像寺创建讲堂碑（辽统和五年）
Stone Tablet Dated to AD 987 Commemorating the Construction of the Lecture Hall at the Qianxiangyoutangsi (Monastery of One Thousand Figures)

081 号石刻局部
Partial View of Carvings No.081

立佛像（左为比丘。编号 032:6-3、032:6-4）
Two Standing Figures (Nos.032:6-3、032:6-4,
Bhiksu at left)

032 号石刻全景
Panoramic View of Carvings No.032

大日如来佛造像（编号075:6-4）
Vairocana Buddha (No. 075:6-4)

局，或单尊或成辅，数目不等。

目前发现的造像均为佛教题材，有佛、菩萨和比丘三种。

佛，占全部造像的绝大多数，体姿分为立姿、坐姿两种，以立姿为主，坐姿又可分为结跏趺坐、倚坐两种。此类造像头部均有头光，大部分为圆形，极少量为桃形，数量一至三重不等；除大日如来等少数几尊佛造像头戴宝冠外，绝大多数头部见有发髻和肉髻，保存较好者可见圆形或扁圆形髻珠以及两眉间的白毫；面型方、圆或长圆；衣纹疏朗，身披袒右式袈裟或双领下垂式大衣，内着僧祇衣，下身着裙；莲座多为单层覆莲，有少数双层仰覆莲座、须弥座等形式；身光仅见于坐姿佛造像。部分造像左手托钵、右手执锡杖或双手托钵，其余造像可辨识的手印有无畏印、智拳印、说法印、莲花合掌印等。

菩萨，可辨识出7尊，均与佛造像共同刊刻于同一岩石表面，应具有组合关系。此类造像全部为立姿，单重头光，头戴宝冠，身体纤秀，衣纹疏朗，臂搭帔帛，宽衣博带。莲座均为单层覆莲。有左手提净瓶者，应为观音菩萨。此类造像集中分布于千像寺遗址的东南和西南部。

比丘，可辨识出10尊，均与佛或佛、菩萨造像共存于同一石块的平坦表面上，可看出具有组合关系。此类造像全部为立姿，单重头光，体态挺拔，身披袒右式袈裟，下身着裙，赤足，单层覆莲莲座。所持的法器，可辨识出持有宝珠的3尊。

另有一类特殊的造像，均为坐姿。从头部观察为佛，刻画较细致，发髻、肉髻、髻珠甚至白毫也清晰可见，但颈部以下是以圆弧形线条组成，简洁、疏朗，不见手足，似为用布将全身裹住一般。此类造像集中分布于千像寺遗址西北方，应具有特殊的含义。

许多造像的旁边刻有带栏框的榜题，但文字大都漫漶不清。可辨识的文字多为"弟子某某为亡母敬造"或"弟子某某敬养"一类的内容，没有发现造像的名称及刊刻造像的时间。

根据造像的特征初步推断，千像寺造像群刊刻

倚坐佛像（编号 088:12-1）
Resting Buddha (No. 088:12-1)

立佛像（编号 059:10-4）
Standing Buddha (No. 059:10-4)

观音菩萨造像（编号 045:8-3）
Guanyin Bodhisattva (No. 045:8-3)

结跏坐佛（编号 069:5-1）
Sitting Buddha with Legs Crossed (No. 69:5-1)

立佛组合像（右侧造像左手托钵，右手执杖。068号石刻）
Grouped Standing Buddhas (No. 068, the figure on the right holding *patra*-bowl
in left hand and *khakkhara*-staff in right hand)

089号石刻全景
Panoramic View
of Carvings No. 089

结跏趺坐佛组合像（编号089:7-1-89:7-6）
Grouped Sitting Buddhas with Legs
Crossed (Nos. 089:7-1-89:7-6)

主佛组合像（中为双手托钵佛造像，编号78:15-9-78:15-11）
Grouped Buddhas (Nos. 78:15-9-78:15-11, the Buddha in the center holding *patra*-bowl with both hands)

立佛像（编号028:7-7）
Standing Buddha (No. 028:7-7)

结跏坐佛像及榜题（编号100:1-1）
Cross-legged Sitting Buddha and Inscriptions (No. 100:1-1)

的时间集中于辽代。

千像寺造像还包括与之相关的辽统和五年（987年）盘山祐唐千像寺创建讲堂碑、辽天庆八年（1118年）经幢，以及寺后洞窟内明代浮雕菩萨和清高宗（乾隆帝）题诗石刻等附属文物。

千像寺造像群，无论是表现形式、榜题内容，还是刊刻技法，都表现出较为明显的民间造像的特点，为目前全国所见的分布面积最广、体量最大的辽代民间石刻造像，其内容新颖，表现独特，在同时期佛教考古、佛教史的研究中占有重要的地位。

（供稿：姜佰国）

The Buddhist figure carvings are identified with an area surrounding the site of the Qianxiangsi (Monastery of One Thousand Figures) which is located north of Lianhe village in Guanzhuang, Jixian County, Tianjin. Lying between the Panshan intrusive hills and plains, the site is 12.5 km southeast of the town of Jixian County at an elevation of between 100 m to 200 m. From 2003 to 2005, the Tianjin Municipal Center for the Preservation of Cultural Heritage carried out field work three times to investigate, survey and draw the rock carvings.

The carvings are all incised either on isolated massive granite rocks or on rock cliffs, with the figures arranged in accordance with the shape of the rocks. The figures are designed either as a singular image or in groups of different sizes, and the grouped figures have different identies, presenting certain interrelationship within the group. For the 535 figures that have so far been identified at 124 rock or cliff locations, the height difference between the highest figure and the lowest one is 95 m, and the size of the spatial distribution is 0.4 sq km.

All the figures are Buddhist motifs. The so far recognized motif types include Buddha, Bodhisattva and Bhiksu. Inferred from the carving of the Vairocana motif, the carvings at Qianxiangsi might be related to the Esoteric Sect of Buddhism. The sizes of the figures are not identical and the shapes also vary. Based on the facial characteristics, hair styles, dress and adornment patterns, and throne morphologies, it is preliminarily inferred that these figures were primarily carved during the Liao period (927-1119). Therefore, the figures at Qianxiangsi are the largest group of Buddhist carvings so far identified in China dating to the Liao period.

The technique and style of the rock carvings at Qianxiangsi present a unique folk tradition. Based on this observation, it is inferred that the carvings were sponsored by common Buddhist donors and believers, representing a strong local belief.

021 号石刻全景
Panoramic View
of Carvings No. 021

长沙坡子街
南宋大型木构建筑遗址

SOUTHERN SONG SITE OF LARGE WOODEN STRUCTURES AT POZIJIE, CHANGSHA, HUNAN

坡子街木构建筑遗址位于长沙市区黄兴路与坡子街交界处的西北角，西距湘江约450米。

2004年8～12月，长沙市文物考古研究所对该遗址进行了抢救性考古发掘。发掘时采取探方发掘法，每个探方10×10米，共布24个探方。

在发现遗迹时，工地已经下挖4米左右，从地表往下，共有19层堆积。木构遗迹叠压在第12层下，打破第13～16层。其中第1、2层为近现代废弃堆积，第3～8层为明清时期堆积，第9～12层出土较多南宋时期衡山窑青瓷片和南宋钱币，第13层出土较多北宋钱币和长沙窑青瓷片。木构遗迹内的淤积土中，也出土了南宋时期的钱币和衡山窑瓷片，因而推断木构建筑的时代为南宋时期。

该建筑遗迹分布范围较大，由三部分组成，一是三角形木构建筑，二是沟槽式木构建筑遗迹。三是券顶式砖砌遗迹。

三角形木构建筑略呈东西向，全长38.1米，从木板形制及构筑方法推测为一地下建筑，其构筑方法是先于平地开挖一条宽2.8、深1.2米的沟，再在沟内铺底板。底板为长方体，长2.5、宽0.65、厚0.15米，距离两端各0.22米处凿有一深0.03米的凹槽，再在上面两侧依次竖侧板，侧板底嵌于凹槽内。侧板均为圆木一侧的1/3，断面呈璜状，长1.6、宽0.66、厚0.2米，两侧均有边搭榫，榫深0.04米，板与板之间相互扣合，最后拼合成长长的三角形人字架木构建筑。侧板依据形制差别及方位可分为两种：南侧边板上端为凹字形，左边为下榫。右边为上榫；北侧边板，上端为凸字形，左边为下榫，右边为上榫。这两种侧板对搭成三角形，下端两侧卡于底板两侧的槽内，这样由东向西，由上至下，整个三角形木构建筑套合严密，制作合理，充分利用力学原理，经久耐用。三角形木构建筑内侧被填土充实。

沟槽式木构建筑遗迹略呈南北向，分为东西两条沟槽式木构建筑遗迹。其构筑方法是先在地上挖一深0.65、宽2.1米的沟，再在沟的东西两

三角形木构建筑（由西向东）
Triangular Wooden Structure (from west to east)

三角形木构建筑与木构沟槽（由东向西）
Triangular Wooden Structure and Wooden Trenches (from east to west)

三角形木构建筑与木构沟槽接合处（由南向北）
Joined Section of Triangular Wooden Structure and Wooden Trench (from south to north)

三角形木构建筑底板（由西向东）
Bottom Board of Triangular Wooden
Structure (from east to west)

南北向两条木构沟槽（由北
向南）
Two Wooden Trenches
in the North-South
Direction (from north
to south)

券顶式砖砌遗迹（由北
向南）
Brick Arch Structure
(from north to south)

壁挡木板，木板内两侧竖对称木桩，其中东侧槽内
为方形木桩，而西侧槽内为圆形木桩，这应是用以
加固壁板。在局部的两木桩间下端又横置一条形
木枋，有的上面有方形或菱形的榫眼。东侧槽残长
17、宽 1.5 米，其壁板厚 0.25～0.27 米。西侧槽
长 32.25、宽 1.5 米，其壁板宽 0.3～0.58 米。其

中在三角形木构建筑相接处，东西两槽间有一同
类型的短槽相接，并且西侧槽在南端转向东，与东
侧槽相连。

　券顶式砖砌遗迹底部叠压在木板遗迹南侧一段
槽内木底板之上，高 2.1、宽 2.9 米，底层竖铺三
层砖，正好砌于木板槽内，之上向外横铺四层砖，

并起券顶，侧墙宽 0.92 米。该建筑的时代应该较大型木构遗迹稍晚。

另外，在木构建筑遗迹西南面，还发现了多处灰坑遗迹。在一个长为 3.6 米的"中"字形灰坑中，置放了两根长圆木和一根短圆木。在遗址内还发现了 30 余口宋至清时期的古井以及大量房屋建筑柱洞等。

由于是配合城市建设的考古发掘，木构建筑遗迹仅发掘了局部，整体布局未完全揭示出来，关于该建筑的性质，从初步发掘情况看，整个木构建筑遗迹内的堆积多为淤泥层，所以推测是与水有关的建筑，据有关专家考证，可能为南宋时期长沙城内的给水系统工程，但也有专家认为是一处大型作坊遗迹。

坡子街大型木构建筑遗迹为长沙地区首次发现，该遗迹处于城市的中心区域，规模大，保存较完整，为城市考古提供了极为宝贵的资料。

（供稿：何旭红 何佳）

From August to December 2004, the Changsha Municipal Institute of Archaeology of Hunan Province excavated a large Southern Song wooden structural site at Pozijie in Changsha City, Hunan Province. The site is widely distributed, comprising mainly of three units including a triangular wooden structure, two trench-like wooden structures, and a brick arch structure.

The triangular wooden structure is orientated approximately in the east-west direction, with a total length of 38.1 m. It is probably an underground structure judging from the board shapes and the method of composition. This structure was composed of the bottom board and side boards, which were clasped to each other, eventually forming a long triangular frame. The trench-like wooden structures, one in the east and the other in the west, are orientated approximately in the north-south direction and connected to the eastern end of the triangular structure. They were composed of wooden boards on two sides, wooden posts, and wooden lintels at the bottom.

The brick arch structure is located in the southeastern part of the site and also extends out of the excavation area. The general shape of this arch structure is that of an underground drainage tunnel.

Furthermore, multiple "ash pits" have been found southwest of the wooden structures. According to some scholars, this site might have been the water supply system inside Changsha City of the Southern Song period; others, however, believe this site was a large workshop of that time.

Wooden structures of this kind have rarely been discovered before, and they are important material for urban archaeological studies.

柱洞内方形白色陶质磉墩
White Square Ceramic Base in Posthole

"中"字形灰坑中放置的圆木
Logs in "中" Shaped Pit

景德镇丽阳乡
元、明瓷窑址考古发掘

EXCAVATION AT THE YUEN-MING KILN SITE
IN LIYANG OF JINGDEZHEN, JIANGXI

景德镇丽阳乡元、明瓷窑址位于江西省景德镇市西南21公里处,遗存主要分布在丽阳乡彭家村瓷器山的西坡和丽阳村碓臼山的南坡。2004年底,窑址遭到盗掘,为保护该窑址并获取科学资料,经国家文物局批准,故宫博物院、江西省文物考古研究所和景德镇陶瓷考古研究所联合组成考古队,于2005年7~11月对景德镇市丽阳乡元、明瓷窑址进行了考古发掘。此次发掘分A、B、C三区,面积为820平方米,发现元、明时期窑炉各一座,出土了许多五代至明清时期的重要瓷器标本,发掘取得重要成果。

元代窑址区(C区)地层堆积共4层,根据层位关系及包含物分析,元代窑址区可分为四期:第一期即为宋~元时期的堆积,包含物中的青白、卵白瓷片是典型的遗物;第二期为元代晚期堆积,包含物均为窑炉废弃后的堆积,出土物主要是未烧熟的成型青釉瓷坯胎。第三期为明代堆积;第四期为近现代堆积。

明代窑址区(A区)地层堆积分5层,根据层位关系及包含物分析,明代窑址区共分三期;第一期为宋元时期堆积,青白、黑釉和卵白釉瓷是该时期的典型遗物;第二期为Y1窑业堆积和废弃后的堆积,属明代早期堆积,出土的青花、仿龙泉、仿哥釉、紫金釉碗、折(弧)腹盘、靶杯是该时期的典型遗物;第三期为近现代堆积,该层由于受到晚期扰乱的缘故,包含物从时代上来说比较混乱,宋

至近现代的遗物都有发现。

发现的遗迹有元代晚期的龙窑窑炉和明代早期的葫芦形窑窑炉各一座。

元代晚期龙窑(Y2)位于丽阳村碓臼山南坡发

元代龙窑全貌(由南向北)
Panoramic View of Yuan Dragon Kiln (from south to north)

元代龙窑窑室内的匣钵柱（由西南
向东北）
Post-like Packed Saggars inside Yuan Dragon Kiln (from
southwest to northeast)

掘区（C区），该窑斜长 24.2 米，坡度 15°，方向
146°。窑门宽 0.8 米，火膛进深 1、高 1、宽 3.5 米。
窑室外弧，最宽处位于窑床中部，宽约 4 米，近火
膛处微内收，宽约 3.4 米。窑尾圆收，没有龙窑常
见的排烟孔设施。

　　明代早期的葫芦形窑炉（Y1）位于彭家村瓷器
山西坡发掘区（A区）的西侧，该窑斜长 11 米，平
均坡度为 9°，方向 258°。窑门宽 0.62 米，火膛进
深 0.69、高 0.57、宽 3.6 米。窑室分前后两室，前
室最宽处约 3.6 米，后室最宽处约 3.4 米，两室束
腰处宽 1.98 米。窑尾圆收。

　　A、C 两区发现的遗物有窑业堆积中的元、明时
期的瓷器标本，亦有早期地层中的宋代瓷器标本。

　　出土瓷器有五代青瓷，宋元青白、黑釉瓷，元
代卵白釉瓷，明代青花、仿龙泉釉、仿哥釉、紫金
釉、白釉瓷器等。器形有碗、盘、靶杯、罐、碟、

瓶、执壶、炉、盏等。

　　从元代窑炉出土的瓷器来看，主要为饼足碗，胎
呈灰色，釉色灰青，有的器外壁下腹处刻有莲瓣纹，
该类产品有元末明初特征。器物均采用单件仰烧，器
底采用泥饼垫烧，其装烧工艺为元代流行的方法。

　　从明代窑炉出土的瓷器来看，虽然釉色品种较
多，但器类以碗、盘、靶杯等日常生活用瓷为主，
青花纹样以云气兰草、缠枝宝相、月梅为主，吉祥
款识"福""寿"有行、楷之分，多书写器物内底，
"梵"字纹样多为写意，一般环饰器物口沿处。仿
龙泉和仿哥釉瓷器从胎釉效果观察，显为工匠刻意
为之，质量效果俱佳。器物均采用单件匣钵仰烧工
艺，圈足较大的器底采用垫砂，圈足较小的器物采
用垫饼垫烧。

　　根据发掘情况，可得出如下结论：

　　1. 元代晚期龙窑窑内未经扰乱的匣钵摞叠成柱

瓷窑窑址 A 区全貌（由西向东）
Full Appearance of District A
of Kiln Site (from west to east)

明代葫芦窑遗址发掘区
情况（由东向西）
Excavation of Ming
Gourd-shaped Kiln
(from east to west)

明代葫芦窑全貌（由西向东）
Full Appearance of Ming
Gourd-shaped Kiln (from
west to east)

明代葫芦窑窑头（由东
向西）
Front of Ming Gourd-
shaped Kiln (from east
to west)

元代青釉刻莲瓣纹碗
Celadon bowl with Incised Lotus Design, Yuan

元代青釉碗
Celadon Bowl, Yuan

元代龙窑遗址出土枢
府釉瓷器
shufu Ware from
the Yuan Dragon
Kiln

状、排列整齐，处于原始装烧状态，窑壁保存较好。从未经扰乱的原状匣钵柱及其排列形式可以看到，匣钵柱之间除了用亚腰形的窑撑保持匣钵柱彼此间的距离外，也有用砖、废匣钵片作窑撑具的现象，从窑撑两端有匣钵接缝印痕看，这些窑撑是当时装窑时用来固定匣钵柱并使之保持间距的泥块，为保持匣钵柱最下面的匣钵平稳，除直接用细泥砂铺垫外，多采用三角形窑垫为支具，或根据需要用废弃窑砖和匣钵片塞垫；每个匣钵内都装有一个规格基本相同的碗，碗底和匣钵之间有垫饼，这种垫饼是在装碗时由窑工把泥饼放在匣钵底部，再把碗坯放在泥饼上并稍用力下压，从而形成平衡。

这座元代晚期龙窑窑炉形制比较特殊，长度较短，火膛较深、大，窑炉左右两壁外弧、炉壁近火膛处微内缩，尾部砌成圆弧形且没有龙窑常见的排烟孔等设施，这几点都是明代典型葫芦形窑的主要特征，加之和明代早期的葫芦形窑炉遗迹同见于一个窑场，这对揭示南方景德镇地区龙窑向葫芦形窑的演变具有重要的启迪意义。

2.葫芦形窑炉是明代景德镇地区流行的瓷器窑炉，以往发现的窑炉保存状况相对较差，关于其烟囱的形制也存在争议。该窑炉的发现不仅可以填补景德镇御窑遗址发现的明初（洪武、永乐时期）葫芦形窑和湖田窑遗址发现的明代中期（弘治时期）葫芦形窑之间的空白，完善葫芦形窑炉的演变序列，也可以印证《天工开物》对葫芦形窑窑炉形制

明代青花炉
Blue-and-white Burner, Ming

明代青花钵
Blue-and-white *bo*-Bowl, Ming

明代青花贯耳瓶
Blue-and-white Vase with
Pierced Handles, Ming

明代青花碗
Blue-and-white Bowl, Ming

明代葫芦窑址出土的仿龙泉釉小盘
Disk with Longquan Style Glaze
from Gourd-shaped Kiln, Ming

明代青花靶杯
Blue-and-white Cup, Ming

明代葫芦窑址出土的仿龙泉釉靶杯
Cup with Longquan Style Glaze
from Gourd-shaped Kiln, Ming

明代仿哥釉碗
Bowl with *ge* Style Glaze, Ming

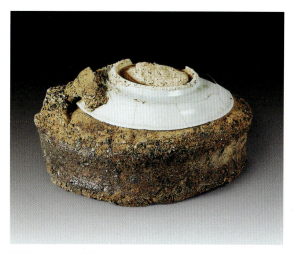

明代白釉盘与匣钵粘连在一起
White Glazed Plate Adhered to Saggar, Ming

的记载。

3.明代早期民窑场仿哥窑和仿龙泉釉瓷器是以往不为人所知的,此次发现丰富了学界对明代早期景德镇地区瓷器釉色品种的认识,而青花、白釉、仿哥釉、仿龙泉釉瓷器器类与造型的统一,又说明在同一座窑场内器物的形制并不因釉色品种的不同而有差异,这对陶瓷考古进行类型学研究尤其具有提示作用。同时上述器物的出土,对研究传世和考古发掘的同时期青瓷、青花、仿龙泉釉和仿哥釉瓷

器的产地均具有标尺意义。

应强调指出的是,对丽阳乡瓷器窑址的考古发掘是考古工作者首次带有课题性质的对景德镇地区元、明时期的民窑遗址进行主动性科学发掘,所取得的收获除可以搞清楚景德镇地区乃至整个江南元明窑炉形制变化的规律,初步建立明代景德镇民窑瓷器的断代编年外,对研究明代民窑生产历史以及对景德镇地区的陶瓷考古也具有推动作用。

(供稿:王上海 江建新 王光尧)

明代葫芦窑址出土的白釉瓷器
White Glazed Porcelain Ware from Gourd-shaped Kiln, Ming

明代紫金釉青花梅月纹碗内部
Inside of Brown Bronze Glazed Blue-and-white Bowl with Plum and Moon Design, Ming

明代紫金釉青花梅月纹碗外底
Outside Base of Brown Bronze Glazed Blue-and-white Bowl with Plum and Moon Design, Ming

Near the Chang River and located 21 km southwest of Jingdezhen, the Ciqishan kiln site is distributed on the western slope of the Ciqishan (Porcelain Mound) and the southern slope of the Duijiushan (Pestle and Mortar Mound) between Pengjiacun village and Liyangcun village in Liyang Town. This kiln had been active from the Five Dynasties to the Ming period, and was a relatively centralized production place outside Jingdezhen. From July to October 2005, archaeologists from the Palace Museum, the Jiangxi Provincial Institute of Archaeology, and the Jingdezhen Institute of Archaeology carried out excavations at the Ciqishan site. They identified one unopened dragon kiln dated to the Yuan period and one gourd-shaped kiln dated to the early Ming dynasty. The structures of the two kilns, therefore, have revealed the transition process of kiln structures in this region from the type of the Yuan dragon kiln to that of the Ming gourd-shaped kiln.

The dragon kiln of the Yuan period is especially important because it is the first porcelain kiln of the Yuan period discovered that had remained unopened after its last firing. Inside the kiln chamber, undisturbed saggars were still piled up as lined up posts, and kiln walls were also well preserved. This intact condition provides solid data for the study and reconstruction of the porcelain economy of the Yuan period with regard to aspects of kiln structure, packing and firing technique, quantity of wares in each firing, and arrangement and allocation of saggars inside the kiln, etc. The unearthed porcelain wares consist of various types, including celadon of the Five Dynasties, bluish white of the Song - Yuan period, celadon of the Yuan period, *shufu* ware as well as many Ming porcelain types, including blue-and-white, wares with Longquan style glaze, wares with the *ge* style glaze, black glaze, white glaze, etc. These archaeologically excavated porcelain remains provide reliable standards for the study of the original production location of contemporary porcelain types.

南京明沐瓒墓的发掘

EXCAVATION OF THE MING TOMB OF MU ZAN IN NANJING

2005年5～6月，为配合南京一开发公司的建设，南京市博物馆和江宁区博物馆联合在南京将军山抢救性发掘了2座明代砖室墓葬，其中一座为沐英四世孙沐瓒夫妇合葬墓。该墓设计独特、功能完善、规模宏大、建筑精良，而且未经盗扰，出土了丰富的陪葬品，是近年来南京地区发现的最具考古价值的明代墓葬之一。

将军山位于南京市南郊的江宁区，是明代开国功臣沐英的家族葬地。沐瓒墓（编号为JJM5）位于将军山西端，与20世纪50年代发掘的沐英墓（编号为JJM1）相距约300米，但分处于两条不同的南北走向的山脊上。该墓四周为坚硬的风化岩层，建造时先在岩层中自上而下垂直地开凿出长方形墓圹，然后再紧贴圹壁修建墓室。该墓的封土层残高约3.5米，在封土层的底部、砖砌墓室的顶部叠铺大量形状不规则、重量皆在百斤以上的大石块，其厚度达1.5米，在墓顶之上形成了坚固的保护层。这些石块与周围岩层的颜色、岩性一致，应是开凿墓圹时取出再加利用的石块。

墓门方向为东偏南36°。墓门前凿出细长的斜坡形墓道，宽约0.8米、总长约52米。在墓道底部偏一侧的位置，开凿有二层台式的排水沟。

墓室全长7.3、宽8.2米，平面近于方形，由甬道、前室和三个后室组成。每个墓室入口均安装有厚重的石门，石门高度、结构相同，由石质门楣、门槛、门扇以及砖砌的门柱组成。前室石门外另有砖砌的七道封门墙，石门上安装铁质铺首衔环，并加有铁锁。门楣内侧中部开凿方形穿孔，从中下插一根铁质插销，顶住门扇。而3个后室石门皆为虚掩，未设锁，门楣上虽凿有穿孔，亦未见有插销。

前室平面呈横长方形，顶部纵向起券成券顶。长7.4、宽2.3、高3.28米。通向后中室的石门两

墓道、排水沟及墓门
Tomb Passage, Drainage Ditch and Chamber Gate

金束发冠
Gold Crown

金簪
Gold Hairpin

金镯
Gold Bracelet

金耳坠
Gold Eardrop

镶嵌红宝石金戒指
Gold Ring Inlaid with Ruby

金链铜镜
Bronze Mirror with Gold Chain

侧，各有一长方形砖砌祭台。三个后室平面呈竖长方形，横向券顶。三室宽度相同，为2.14米。墓室长度均为4.2米，但由于后壁龛深度的不同而导致总长有差异。其中右室最长，总长5.04米，中室总长4.7米，左室总长4.6米。由于墓室紧贴墓圹修建，出现这种情况应是墓圹开凿得不甚规整所致的。中室高2.96米，比左、右两室各高出5厘米。后室的后壁皆建有拱形壁龛。中室两侧前部各设一方形穿洞，后部各设一拱形穿洞，与左、右两室相通。而左室左壁、右室右壁与拱形穿洞对应的位置则各设一拱形壁龛。壁龛的后壁均无砖，直接以墓圹石壁作为后壁。三个后室内中间皆设有长方形砖砌棺床，长约2.3、宽约1、高约0.2米，用砖砌出四周边框，框内填土。前、后室墓壁皆用四层砖砌就，厚达0.5米，除券顶部分使用竖砖外，其余部分皆用平砖上砌。墓底铺地砖一层。

墓葬未遭盗扰，3具棺木皆朽，残存的部分棺板散落于棺床四周。人骨亦大部不存。出土的随葬器物以金银器和锡器为主，另有少量玉器、陶器、铜器和铁器。

随葬器物集中放置于前室祭台、三个后室的棺床及壁龛内。前室石门左侧放置一直径约80厘米的陶缸；左侧祭台上放置一具由铜、铁片制作的铠甲，甲上放置一顶铜、铁质地的凤翅头盔，已散乱。右侧祭台上置铁剑一把，并有带盖罐、瓠、

炉、烛台等锡质祭器。

中室棺床上出土有金冠、银串珠、玛瑙珠串、金链铜镜、玉带、龙头金镯、镶红宝石金饰件及金扣等。特别是在中室棺床上，从头至脚覆盖着近50枚直径大、分量重的金、银冥币，而绝大多数为金冥币，其中最重的金币单枚重量达350余克。这些金、银冥币上皆有小孔，推测它们原应是缝制固定于被服上，然后再覆盖在尸体表面的。

在左室棺床头部位置出土了20余枚用极细金丝绞结成的女性佩戴的金钿花形装饰，其制作工艺十分精湛。此外还出土了金珠链、金链铜镜、龙头金镯，以及5枚分别镶有红、蓝宝石和绿松石的金戒指等。左室棺床从头至脚覆盖着90余枚直径大、分量重的金、银冥币，但与中室不同的是，其以银币为主，金币仅占三分之一。

右室棺床上主要出土金簪、镶玉嵌红宝石金耳环、镶红宝石金戒指等，棺床上还出土了近50枚金、银冥币，其中金、银币各占一半，但无论是直径还是重量都无法与其他两室出土的金、银冥币相比。在三座后室的壁龛和洞龛中主要放置了锡质的灶、鼎、瓠、烛、台、盘、壶、杯以及小陶罐、铜匙等。

墓志共出土三合，呈"品"字形竖直放置于前室石门之外，并被仔细地埋藏于封门墙内。每合墓志皆用铁箍箍紧。从墓志记载得知，墓主人为"大

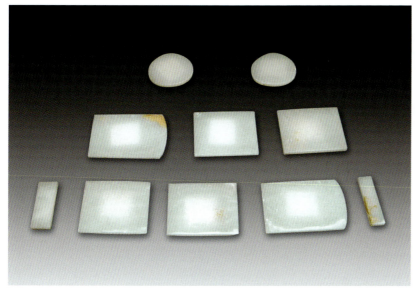

玉带
Jade Plaque

锡瓠
Tin *gu*

明都督同知副总兵"沐瓒，以及他的正妻贾氏和侧室刘氏。三合墓志的摆放位置与墓主的埋葬位置相对应——摆放于前部正中的是沐瓒墓志，表明中室墓主为沐瓒；左后部放置的是贾氏墓志，表明左室墓主为贾氏；右后部放置的为刘氏墓志，对应右室墓主。

沐瓒为沐英第三子沐昂之孙。明天顺年间，由于承袭黔国公爵位的沐琮年幼，经朝廷批准，由沐瓒代镇云南，直至成化三年，琮始之镇，而以瓒为副总兵，移镇金齿。《明史》记载，沐瓒"居七年，先后讨平沾禄诸寨及土官之构兵者，降思卜发，勒还诸蛮侵地。功多，然颇黩货。"沐琮死后，由于无子，朝廷"以瓒孙昆嗣"。其后黔国公的爵位一直由沐瓒这一支承袭，直至明亡。

从20世纪50年代起，南京市博物馆已先后在将军山地区发掘了属于明代早期的沐英、其子沐晟墓，属于明代晚期的沐英九世孙沐昌祚、十世孙沐璘墓。此次发掘是将军山沐氏家族墓葬区中第5个重要发现，其时代为明代中期。

沐瓒墓的发现为进一步了解将军山沐氏家族墓地的分布范围、排列规律、丧葬特征提供了新资料。

另外，距离沐瓒墓约20米处，还发现一座明代单室券顶砖墓（编号为JJM6）。M6长2.3、宽1.03、高1.2米，墓主为女性，棺木已朽。但骨架保存较好。出土随葬品有金包髻、金簪、金戒指、金耳环、银手镯、铜镜、青花瓷罐、买地券等。此墓虽然规模较小，且未出土墓志，但从墓葬形制及出土遗物判断，其时代为明代中晚期。墓主也应为沐氏家族成员。

（供稿：华国荣 祁海宁 张金喜）

金冥钱
Gold Funerary Money

银冥钱
Silver Funerary Money

The tomb of Mu Zan is located on the hill named Jiangjunshan in Jiangning District, Nanjing City, Jiangsu Province. During May and June 2005, the Museum of Nanjing carried out a rescue excavation of the tomb.

The tomb consists of a passage and four chambers. The tomb passage, measuring over 30 m in length and around 0.7 m in width, was cut into hard rocks and designed with a drainage ditch at the bottom. Measuring 7.3 m in total length and 8.2 m in width, the four tomb chambers, one at the front and three at the back, were all installed with a thick and heavy stone gate. Outside the stone gate of the front chamber, seven blocking walls were also built, and the gate was attached with a lock outside and blocked with an iron bar inside. The top of the tomb was fully covered by large rocks 1.5 m thick, each rock weighing over 50 kg.

Over 340 funerary items were unearthed from the tomb, including mainly gold, silver and tin wares but also some jade, pottery, bronze and iron items in small amounts. As the tomb had not been disturbed in the past, the funerary goods therefore basically remained in their original locations.

According to the unearthed epitaph, the occupants of the tomb were Mu Zan, the fourth-generation grandson of Mu Ying, a meritorious founding general of the Ming dynasty, and Mu Zan' two wives, Lady Jia and Lady Liu. Mu Zan in his life was a high ranking general at the provincial level and once managed military and administrative affairs in today's Yunnan area on behalf of Duke Qian State. Since the 1950s, the Museum of Nanjing has unearthed four tombs of Mu Ying and his offspring in the Jiangjunshan area, and the 2005 excavation is the fifth discovery of a Mu family tomb.

长沙蚂蚁山一号明墓的发掘

EXCAVATION OF MING TOMB NO. 1 AT MAYISHAN IN CHANGSHA, HUNAN

2005年4~9月，长沙市文物考古研究所及望城县文物管理所联合对位于湖南省长沙市望城县的蚂蚁山一号大墓进行了抢救性考古发掘。

该墓葬为一大型砖室券顶墓，由墓道、前室、后室以及东、西两个侧室构成，券顶共有20层青砖。墓葬总长19米，最宽处14.5米。

墓道为竖穴式，墓道内填土为夯筑，共有23层，其内自上而下发现有石质建筑、"十"字形建筑及井状建筑等少见的古代葬制。在石质建筑内置一石质喇嘛塔，塔内发现有数十册纸质书籍。现已揭取出一本书的封面，书名为《太上洞玄灵宝高上玉皇本行集经》，为道家经书，系金粉楷书抄写。"十"字形建筑为砖石结合堆砌而成，在该建筑槽内，发现一个铜碗和一面铜镜。井状遗迹位于墓道底部正中心，圆形凹底。

蚂蚁山一号墓共出土金、银、铜、铁、瓷、石、木质等各类重要文物146件，墓主人为谷王乳母张妙寿，卒于明永乐十一年（1413年）。

该墓的建造形制，融佛、道思想于一体，对于研究明朝早期的宗教史、思想史、丧葬史等均具有重要的学术意义。

蚂蚁山一号明墓为一座大型砖室券顶墓，位于湖南省长沙市望城县含浦镇白鹤社区茶园冲组。该墓发现于2005年4月，4~9月，长沙市文物考古研究所及望城县文物管理所联合对该墓进行了考古发掘。

墓葬位于山体正中，呈南北向分布，形制大体呈"中"字形结构，由墓道、前室、后室以及东西侧室5个部分组成。全长19、宽14.5、（残）深7.12米。

墓葬封土由于基建破坏，仅存南端一小部分。墓道位于墓葬的南端，竖穴式，南北长6.4、东西宽5.16米。墓道内填土共23层，系夯筑而成，非常坚固。其内自上而下发现有石质建筑、"十"字形建筑及井状建筑。

石质建筑顶部呈塔状，其下为圆柱体，内空，下有一方形底座，全部由石块垒砌而成，直径2.2、通高2.14米。在石质建筑之中，有一直径为0.96米的圆柱形空洞，里面放置一件精美的石质喇嘛塔。塔高156厘米，在塔的覆钵内发现一件漆函，内装有数十册纸质书籍。书籍长17.2、宽8厘米。现在揭取出一本书的封面，书名为《太上洞玄灵宝高上玉皇本行集经》，为道家经书，用金粉楷书抄写。该批书籍保存状况良好，字迹非常工整清晰。

"十"字形建筑位于墓道底部南端正中，叠压在第22层下，为砖石结合堆砌而成的建筑，共有两层，中间纵横轴线上用青石铺成"十"字形，四角为青砖砌成的方形砖墩。在该建筑中间槽内，发现一件铜碗和一面铜镜。

井状建筑位于墓道底部正中，圆形竖穴凹底，口径1.3、深2.1米。井内填土为疏松的红色土，井底横置一个长52厘米的木桩。

整个墓室由前室、后室以及东、西两个侧室构成，均为青石券顶。南北长13.5、东西宽9.3米。

蚂蚁山一号墓全景
Comprehensive View of
Mayishan Tomb No.1

墓道内圆形石塔建筑中出土
石质佛塔
Stone lama Pagoda from
Round Stone Structure
inside Tomb Passage

券顶青砖砌法为一横一竖，共有20层，其中第5～6层为松香砂石砖层，即用松香、砂石粘合制成，状似砖块，再一块块垒砌成墙，十分严密、坚固，可起防水、防潮及防盗等功用。在后室券顶东北侧发现一盗洞，墓葬各室均已被盗扰。

封门墙位于南墙正中，宽3.2、高1.56米，由外往内共12层砖，第4层为松香砂石砖层。

墓葬前室南北长2.5、东西宽3.24、高3.06米。

东西两侧室对称分布，位于前室两侧。两侧室均有青砖封门墙。侧室长3.04、宽1.44、高1.36米，其内东西向各放置一口红漆木棺。

墓葬前、后室之间有隔墙及石门，隔墙为3层青砖，石门为双扇内开，有门楣、门梁及门地辐。后室长5.24、宽3.24、高3.06米。葬具为一棺一

墓道底部圆形竖井及墓室南面
封门墙
Round Vertical Well at
Passage's Bottom and
Gate-blocking Wall at South
Side of Tomb Chamber

墓道底部十字形建筑俯视
Top View of Cross-shaped
Structure at Lower Part of
Tomb Passage

前室遗物分布
Distribution of Objects
in Front Chamber

石塔覆钵内出土漆函
Lacquered Book Box from the Lidded
bo-bowl in Stone Pagoda

漆函内放置的经书
Taoist Book from
Lacquered Box

张氏墓志盖
Cover of Lady Zhang's Epitaph Box

椁，棺外黑漆内红漆，长2.43、宽0.92、高1.03米。椁呈长方体，外表髹黑漆，长2.97、宽1.6、高1.68米。椁下南北向平铺两块青石条，以承垫棺椁。整个墓室底部平整，为三砂板结层，无铺地砖。

蚂蚁山一号墓共出土金、银、铜、铁、瓷、石及木质等各类重要文物146件（书籍除外），计有墓志、金铃、金锭、圆形金箔片、银钱币、银勺状器、银筷状器、铜筷状器、铜盘、铜杯、铜丝、玛瑙珠、铁剪、铁板、漆木梳、木俑、木簪、木珠、木方座、酱釉大缸等。

墓志置于前室，由墓志盖、墓志、墓志底座组成。墓志盖阴刻"张氏妙寿之墓"6字，篆体。墓志刻字为方正楷体，记载墓主为谷王乳母张妙寿，明洪武十二年（1379年）入宫，卒于永乐十一年（1413年），享年70岁。

在墓道中发掘的圆形石质建筑、"十"字形砖石建筑、圆形竖井等均为国内罕见的古代葬制。

该墓下葬年代为明代早期，其建造形制及随葬物，融佛、道思想于一体，对于研究明朝的宗教史、思想史、丧葬史等均具有重要的学术意义。

（供稿：黄朴华 何佳）

From April to September 2005, the Changsha Municipal Institute of Archaeology and the Wangcheng County Office of Cultural Heritage jointly carried out a rescue excavation at Mayishan Tomb No. 1 in Wangcheng County of Changsha City, Hunan Province.

Mayishan Tomb No.1 is a large arch-roofed brick grave, composed of a passage, a front chamber, a rear chamber and two side chambers on the eastern and western sides. The arch roof was built up with 20 layers of gray bricks. The grave is 19 m in total length and 14.5 m in maximum width.

The passage is a vertical shaft filled with 23 layers of rammed earth. Within the passage, a series of rarely seen structures were discovered from the top to the bottom, including a round stone tower, a cross-shaped feature, and a well-shaped feature. Inside the round stone structure, a stone *lama* pagoda was placed; inside the stone pagoda, scores of paper books were stored. The cover page of one of the books has been retrieved, which shows the book title "*taishang tongxuan lingbao gaoshang yuhuang benxing jijing*" (Book of Preexistent Activities of the Supreme Jade Emperor). This is a book of Taoism that was written with gold powder in the *kai* regular script. The cross-shaped structure was built with bricks and stones. Inside the groove of this structure, a bronze bowl and a bronze mirror were found. The well-shaped structure is located at the center of the passage's bottom, and has a round shape and a depressed base.

146 objects have been unearthed from Mayishan Tomb No.1, including various material types such as gold, silver, bronze, iron, porcelain, stone, wood, etc. The occupant of the tomb is Lady Zhang Miaoshou, who was a nanny of King Gu and died in the 11th Year of the Yongle Reign of the Ming dynasty (AD 1413).

The structure and arrangement of Mayishan Tomb No. 1 reflect the combined Buddhist and Taoist ideas. This discovery therefore is academically significant for the study of the history of religion, the history of thought, and the history of mortuary practice of the early Ming period.

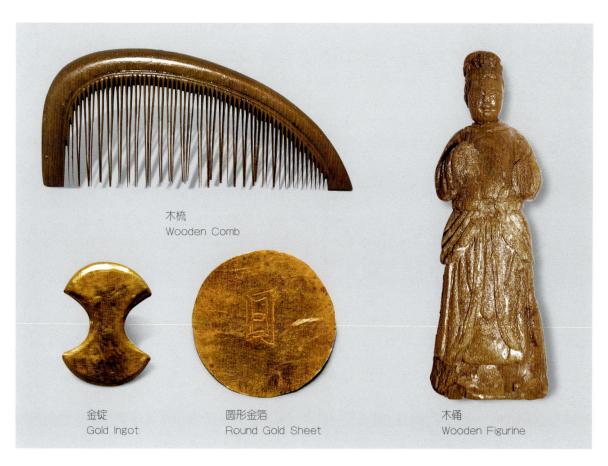

木梳
Wooden Comb

金锭
Gold Ingot

圆形金箔
Round Gold Sheet

木俑
Wooden Figurine

福建东海平潭碗礁1号沉船遗址抢救性发掘

RESCUE EXCAVATION AT THE SITE OF SUNKEN SHIP NO. 1 AT WANJIAO REEF OF PINGTAN IN THE EAST CHINA SEA, FUJIAN

东海平潭碗礁Ⅰ号沉船遗址位于福建省福州市平潭县屿头乡北侧五州群礁的中心——碗礁附近。遗址所在海域水深13～15米，海底为含沙淤泥土质，水下能见度基本保持在0.1～0.5米。该遗址2005年6月下旬被当地渔民发现即遭大规模盗掘。7月上旬国家文物局批准，实施抢救性发掘，至10月15日完成了预定的第一阶段沉船遗址及周边范围水下发掘清理工作。

发掘工作由中国国家博物馆水下考古研究中心组织，组成"碗礁Ⅰ号沉船水下考古队"，人员分别来自福建省、辽宁省、安徽省、海南省、江西省、湖北省、广西省、青岛市、宁波市、厦门大学等地区和部门，共34名水下考古专业人员。

本次抢救性发掘分为两个阶段进行。第一阶段完成沉船内部承载物和遗址周围的发掘清理。第二阶段完成船体测量发掘及相关的文物保护工作。

在全面发掘开始前，首先清理被盗掘者遗弃在沉船遗址的残损瓷器并探摸船体的破损情况。在沉船遗址东西两侧设立基点，布设基线。沿基线两侧进行发掘清理，利用水下摄像和照相设备记录遗址表面的堆积，通过人工采用二维测量方式，记录在遗址表面的相对位置，然后进行发掘清理。采取人工或机械方式提升出水。共发掘清理残损瓷器近3000件，多为青花罐、五彩罐、花觚、大盘等大型器物。被盗掘遗址总长度达6.9米，宽4米，横跨六个船舱位。根据盗掘面积和船舱的位置分析，被盗掘的文物数量不少于2万件，损失非常惊人。

虽然遗址在发现之初即遭盗掘，但都集中在船体的中间部分，根据探摸资料分析，在船的东部和西部尚有部分未被破坏的船舱掩埋在淤泥之下，覆盖在遗址表面的淤泥平均高度约0.5米。清淤工作采用气升式抽泥法，利用空气压缩机将高压空气直接压入水下抽泥管中，利用气压差原理，将附着在遗址上方和周围的淤泥提升到水面工作船，为防止小件文物的遗失，在工作船设立过滤设施。

原计划发掘工作采用全面揭露方式，在遗址上布设2×2米探方，进行全面测量、记录和发掘清理。但盗掘分子利用台风"海棠"来临期间工作船和负责现场保卫的武警快艇回港避风的时机，冒10级大风，利用黑夜做掩护，进行疯狂盗掘。根据

水下工作
Working under Water

水下文物
Underwater Artifacts

情况的严重性，考古队果断改变原有计划，采用分区分段发掘的方式，将沉船遗址分为东西两个区域，逐舱进行清理发掘，并很快在东西两个区域发现未被破坏的船舱。

沉船承载物主要以瓷器为主，瓷器为清代康熙中期景德镇民窑产品，累计出水17000余件。主要器形有将军罐、大盘、花觚、尊、香炉、罐、碗、深腹杯、中盘、器盖、浅腹碗、小盘、小碗、小杯、

出水瓷器
Porcelain Wares Out of Water

青花云间
Blue-and-white *yunjian*
Cylindrical Stand with Lid

青花花卉纹将军罐
Porcelain Wares Out of Water:
Blue-and-white *jiangjun guan*-jars
with Flower Design

青花四开光人物盖罐
Blue-and-white Lidded *guan*-jar with Four-paneled Portraiture Design

冰梅纹盘
Pan-plate with Plum Design

汝窑洗
Washer with *ru* Kiln Glaze Style

粉盒、笔筒、小瓶、小盏、洗等，另外还发现有石质砚台、铜钱和铜锁等。

　　因沉船遗址埋藏较浅，发现之初遭到大规模盗掘，船体本身同样遭受严重破坏。船体残长13.5、残宽3、残高1米。在船体的西南部，发现一根木头，周长0.77、宽0.22、高0.26米，剖面呈"凸"字形，推测为船体的龙骨部分。沉船方向基本为东西向，船头向东，船体沉态倾斜，南高北低，倾斜

角度为41°。该沉船遗址残存16个舱位，多数隔舱板遭到破坏。船艏部分三个舱位之间距离较窄，宽度0.3~0.6米，其他舱位宽度基本为0.9米，只有东六舱宽度为1.34米。

　　东一、二舱舱位距离较窄，未发现器物。其余各舱位均有发现，但各舱位所载瓷器有差异。沉船遗址的东部区域的船舱部分主要装载大型立体器物。东三到东七舱，以将军罐、青花罐、五彩罐、

花瓶、香炉等大件器物为主。以东四舱为例，该舱以青花罐和五彩罐为主，已知是2或3层，罐子首尾相接。东七舱也是上下两层，上层为平放的将军罐，抵在隔舱板之间，下层是青花罐或五彩罐。西部区域的船舱部分主要装载有碗、五彩杯、五彩盘、青花盘、葫芦瓶、青花杯等器物。西一舱以装载青花杯和五彩杯为主，成摞平行码放，高至5层，保持着装载时的原貌，杯与杯之间发现有充当保护性填充物的稻壳和麻制绳索残段。西二舱主要是青花盘和五彩杯。西三舱有碗、杯、小盘、五彩盘。西四舱主要有杯、碗、五彩盘、青花大盘。西五舱主要有碗、杯、小盘、盘、葫芦瓶。西六舱主要有盘、碗、杯、碟、葫芦瓶等。西七舱主要有碗、盘等。

在西三、六、七舱内，均发现有木桶。木桶直接放在船底，桶内装有瓷器，已知的有大盘、五彩杯、葫芦瓶等。桶底直径0.7，残高0.7米。

在西六、七舱的底部发现有压舱石，多为小型鹅卵石，直径4~6厘米，数量较多，多位于船舱的南部。由于船下沉过程中，船体发生倾斜，大量文物散落在船体外侧。在船艏南侧发现有青花罐和将军罐。在船体中部南侧1米处，发现有大量的碗、盘、杯、碟。在船艉西南侧发现大量的碗、盘、碟、花瓶、罐、粉盒等，同时出水的还有一枚 "顺治通宝"以及瓷制镇纸、石质砚台、青釉碗、铜锁等。在船体北侧同样发现有盘、碗等少量瓷器。

福建"东海平潭碗礁I号"沉船遗址抢救性发掘工作，无疑有力推动了水下文物普查工作和海上丝绸之路、古代造船史、古陶瓷史等方面的研究。"碗礁I号"沉船遗址地处传统的海上丝绸之路航线，北至长江流域和北方各港口，南达泉州、广州等贸易港口远至台湾和东南亚地区，是南北海上贸易的必经之路，目前仍是5000吨级以下船舶的通行航线。根据已掌握的水下遗址线索显示，在北至连江海域南到莆田海域有7处水下遗址，其中距"碗礁I号"最近的遗址不足500米，以上大部分遗址遭到盗掘，在如此不大的海域内发现众多的水下遗址，在全国沿海地区尚属首次。加强对水下文化遗产的保护措施，加快水下考古调查发掘，已是当务之急。

（供稿：赵嘉斌 李滨 徐海滨）

The site of "Sunken Ship No. 1 at Wanjiao Reef of Pingtan in the East China Sea" is located near Wanjiao reef, the center of the Wuzhou Reef Complex north of Yutou Town, Pingtan County, Fuzhou City, Fujian Province. The depth of the sea area at the site is between 13 m to 15 m. The sea bed is a deposition of sandy silt, and the visibility usually varies from 0.1 m to 0.5 m. This site was accidentally found and severely hunted by local fishermen in late June 2005. With the permission of the State Administration of Cultural Heritage issued in early July 2005, the Underwater Archaeological Research Center of the National Museum of China carried out the underwater rescue excavation at the sunken ship site and surrounding sea area, and completed Phase 1 of the project by 15 October 2005.

The main shipment of the sunken ship was porcelain wares made by folk kilns in Jingdezhen during the middle Kangxi Reign of the Qing dynasty. Of the over 17,000 objects collected from the water, the major types include the *jiangjun* (General, large) guan-jar, large *pan*-plate, *hu*-vase, zun-urn, incense burner, *guan*-jar, *wan*-bowl, deep-bellied cup, mid-sized *pan*-plate, lid, shallow-bellied *wan*-bowl, small *pan*-dish, small *wan*-bowl, small cup, powder box, brush holder, small vase, *zhan*-tea cup, washer, etc. Other collected object types include inkstone, bronze coinage, and bronze lock.

The preservation condition of the ship has been revealed through the excavation. As the sunken ship was covered shallowly, the main body of the ship was severely damaged. The remaining frame of the ship measures 13.5 m long, 3 m wide, and 1 m high. In the southwestern part of the ship, a wooden object was found with a 凸 shaped section, measuring 0.77 m in perimeter, 0.22 m in width, 0.26 m in height. This wooden object is probably a part of the keel of the ship frame. The orientation of the sunken ship is approximately in the east-west direction, with its head towards the east. The ship is currently tilted at 41 degrees, inclined from south to north. Its bones remain in the ship, and most of the division plates have been damaged.

The rescue excavation is planned to be continued in 2006.